THE WORD IS FLESH AND BLOOD

This book is offered to Wilfrid J. Harrington, OP,
to mark his eighty-fifth birthday

The Word is Flesh and Blood

The Eucharist and Sacred Scripture

Edited by

Vivian Boland OP

&

Thomas McCarthy OP

DOMINICAN PUBLICATIONS
2012

First published (2012) by
Dominican Publications
42 Parnell Square
Dublin I

ISBN 978-1-905604-16-6

Cover and book design by
Bill Bolger

Printed by
Naas Printing, Naas, Co. Kildare
Ireland

ACKNOWLEDGEMENTS

The publishers gratefully acknowledge permission to reproduce the icons
commissioned with the 2012 International Eucharistic Congress
in mind: the image on our cover ('Elijah and the Raven') is from
an icon written by Colette Clarke. Further details on p 208. Gratitude is
expressed also to Pat Lucey, OP, for permission to reproduce the photograph
of Wilfrid J. Harrington, OP.

The editors are deeply grateful also to
Deirdre Hetherington
Conor McDonough OP
Miriam Tracey MSHR

'Did not our hearts burn within us
while he talked to us on the road,
while he opened to us the scriptures?'
– Luke 24:32

Contents

Wilfrid J. Harrington, Scholar and Friend

MICHAEL GLAZIER

WILFRID J. HARRINGTON OP is a man of deep convictions, one who is studious yet wears his learning lightly; a man of many friendships, some spanning many decades; a scholar who is aware that the Bible poses numerous and unending challenges; and he has spent his life exploring its message and untangling its complexity. A group of scholars have written this book to honour his achievements; but it is not a *Festschrift* that marks the end of a career. Far from it: other books are in the pipeline – to add to more than fifty already published. Nor has Wilfrid any intention of ending his teaching assignments in Dublin and in America.

In the late 1950s, Wilfrid began to publish articles on Scripture, encouraged, as he likes to recall, by one of his students, a fellow Corkman called Jerome Murphy-O'Connor. In 1963 Wilfrid's writing career started in earnest, in Manhattan, when someone sent me a batch of pamphlets written by him on the four gospels. I thought they should appear as a book but the problem was to interest a suitable publisher. I called a very serious and studious editor and he promised to read the pamphlets. A few weeks later he called and suggested that we meet at *The Brittany* on the west side of New York City. This was a restaurant known for its rural French cuisine, and seasoned drinkers swore that its 'Southern Comfort Manhattan' was the best in the city. The serious editor and I had a couple of drinks and I futilely suggested that we order dinner and told him that wise men had sworn that the 'Southern Comfort Manhattan' was the enemy of tomorrow. Early the following morning I got a tired and dour call from the editor stating, very bluntly, that all agreements made at *The Brittany* were null and void. He forgot that the possible book was never discussed.

Later that day, when his health was much improved, he called again and almost cheerfully told me he would gladly publish the Harrington book and it would bear the title *Explaining the Gospels*.

Wilfrid Harrington's first book was on its way in America and it was a great success, which encouraged him to accept an invitation from Priory Press to write a commentary for the Bible. *Record of Revelation* was published in three volumes in 1963. The trilogy was translated into French, Spanish, German, Italian, Polish and Croatian. When Priory Press went out of business, Alba House published another hardback edition, but it became obvious that it should be published in paperback to reach a wide student market. Alba House negotiated with Doubleday's prestige Image Books series which issued a paper book edition with a new title, *Key to the Bible*, and it had a great academic reception. Wilfrid Harrington became known as an author who understood the mind and needs of students. In 1978, when Bible study groups were proliferating, his *New Guide to Reading and Studying the Bible* was used by groups all over North America.

Wilfrid is a liturgical man and is keenly interested in the scriptural readings in the liturgy. He wrote two three-volume studies on the liturgical readings: *The Gracious Word* and *The Saving Word*; and he also published studies of the four Evangelists: *Mark, Realistic Theologian*; *Matthew, Sage Theologian*; *Luke, Gracious Theologian*; and *John, Spiritual Theologian*. A glance at the bibliography at the end of this book helps one appreciate the wide variety and scope of his biblical writing.

After her coronation in 1558 Queen Elizabeth I, anxious to convert the Gaelic-speaking Irish from Catholicism to Protestantism, decreed that the New Testament should be translated into Gaelic and contributed a printing press and type fonts to print the book. She evidently did not appreciate the difficulty of a task that was only completed in 1603, the year of her death. In the following centuries Protestant scholars translated the New Testament, and, less often, the entire Bible into Gaelic (Irish). In 1981 the complete Bible was published in this language by Maynooth University: Wilfrid Harrington (*Wilfrid O hUrdail*) was among the scholars who contributed to *An Bíobla Naofa*.

Recently an administrator in St Michael's College in Vermont was asked how long Wilfrid Harrington had taught in the college's summer school. He paused, and then opined, 'Harrington is like the library. He seems to be around forever'. Actually it was Paul Couture SSE, the director of the summer school at St Michaels's College run by the Edmundites, who in 1964 invited Wilfrid to teach the New Testament courses. Every year since then he has been invited back, and he was recently told to keep coming back 'until his summers run out'. He makes a point of knowing every pupil in his class, and it is safe to guess that, over the years, Wilfrid never gave a failing grade to any pupil. After finishing at St Michael's, Wilfrid used to give a retreat to a community of enclosed nuns (during the retreats he wrote *Come, Lord Jesus: a Biblical Retreat*) and then he used to visit us to take it easy after a working summer.

One evening he mentioned how grateful he was for the stipend that the enclosed nuns gave him. I jokingly said that the good nuns were breaking all the minimum wage laws and suggested that he do a little work in my publishing company: and since then Wilfrid has been a regular visitor before he sets off for St Michael's each year. Joan, my wife, says he is the ideal guest. He rises every morning before 5:30, fixes his breakfast and sets out on a very long walk past the groves and lakes which beautify the small town (pop. 1,200) noted for its great book shops, good bars, art stores and genial people.

One afternoon in 1978 he surprised me by asking why my company did not publish Catholic books. I told him that the company was set up to publish legal history and congressional studies in series rather than individual books. He suggested that I should consider publishing a multi-volume commentary on the New Testament with the title *New Testament Message* and said he would co-edit the series if I found an American biblical scholar who would co-edit with him. A few weeks later I was in New York and I decided to ask Raymond Brown SS to see me. He valued his time and rationed it sparingly. He told me to meet him at 9 am for a brief meting at Union Theological Seminary. I told him I intended to publish a new New Testament commentary. He said he thought it was an opportune idea, and said that Donald Senior CP, whom he greatly respected, would make the ideal American co-editor. Harrington and Senior worked wonderfully and constructively together as editors, and their project was published in record time.

Wilfrid Harrington believes that America has become the centre of Catholic biblical research, and many of the scholars who write in this volume have contributed significantly to making it and keeping it so. But the list of contributors to this volume shows that biblical studies are alive and well in other parts of the world, not least in Ireland, in Australia, and among Wilfrid's Dominican brothers and sisters. This book is a fitting tribute to Wilfrid Harrington, honouring him and his remarkable contributions (thus far!) to biblical scholarship, pastoral liturgy and the preaching of the Gospel. The chapters follow the order of the Mass, using the Bible to illustrate aspects of the liturgy and turning to the liturgy to highlight biblical themes. It will be of interest therefore far beyond the academic community and should prove very useful for the Church at large. In this it carries on the biblical and liturgical apostolate that has been Wilfrid's life's work.

Part One

ASSEMBLY

Our Lady of Refuge and St John

CHAPTER ONE

The Bible and the Eucharist

THOMAS McCARTHY OP

Let us run with perseverance the race set before us, looking to Jesus
the pioneer and perfecter of our faith, who for the sake of the joy
that was set before him endured the cross, disregarding its shame,
and has taken his seat at the right hand of the throne of God.

– cf Hebrews 12:1f

THE 'RACE' PROPOSED to those who first listened to this early
Christian homily is the very same course pursued by disciples
today. We may say it is a relay race, in the course of which a baton
composed of tradition and scripture is passed from one participant
to the next, intact – perhaps even enhanced. It is a lengthy stretch:
enduring not only beyond the lifespan of any disciple but as long
as the range of the New Covenant, from Last Supper to Last Day.

As Luke reaches the deadly and life-giving climax of his Gospel,
he reports Jesus' words, and the Eucharistic community has
remembered them ever since: 'This cup that is poured out for you
is the new covenant in my blood' (Lk 22:20). Remembering these
poignant words – spoken the night the Lord was betrayed by an
apostle – the Church remains loyal to an instruction issued on the
same occasion: 'Do this in remembrance of me' (Lk 22:19). (Gregory
Dix wonders, 'Was ever another command so obeyed'?[1]) Fidelity
to that directive, found also in other early Christian texts besides
the New Testament, involves taking and consecrating a loaf of
bread and a cup of wine, recognizing them as the Lord's body and
blood, the sacrificial 'ink' that signed the New Covenant.

1. *The Shape of the Liturgy*, Westminster, Dacre, 1945, 744.

Setting the scene for this book, I will reflect on the links that bind Bible and Eucharist, before noting how the essays between these covers examine central features of this unbreakable bond.

I: 'ALL ARE ASSEMBLING AND COMING TOWARDS YOU' (Is 60:4)

As a risen Zion can welcome her children home in this prophetic text, so the risen Christ can summon his disciples to 'Come and have breakfast!' (Jn 21:12). A notable participant in the early development of Christian life speaks of 'all who live in cities or in the country gather[ing] in one place ... on the day called Sunday'.[2] Justin's witness is to a pattern that had become, and was to remain, characteristic of Christian practice. Once they gather, the disciples recall the teaching of Jesus and his meaning. They actually participate in his life-giving sacrifice by means of the sacrament. And they come to realize how central, for acquiring a sense of their own new and redeemed life, is a recognition of Jesus' dedication to the welfare of all men and women. It is in fact the risen Lord who celebrates and is the true 'sense' of the Eucharistic assembly.

Once the disciples are assembled, the reality of wrongdoing is acknowledged. Gratitude for the Lord's mercy is expressed, together with the Church's awareness of standing constantly in need of it. What is noteworthy is that many biblical texts deal also with the aftermath of sin, indeed its defeat in Christ's life and death – leading to lives that are renewed and potentially rebuilt. New Testament texts tell of death's final destruction – the emergence, that is, of a life to outstrip what is mortal. Trepidation in hearts aware of sin is overcome now by the mercy of Christ ('take heart, your sins are forgiven' – Mt 9:2), inspiring confidence to sing glory to God and express heartfelt desires and prayers, collectively, in the Spirit of Jesus who, when leaving Jericho, called a man over and asked him, 'What do you want me to do for you?' (Mk 10:51).

II: 'MAKE THE PEOPLE SIT DOWN' (cf Mk 6:39)

When disciples are gathered 'the memoirs of the apostles or the writings of the prophets are read'.[3] In biblical texts, from Old

2. Justin, *First Apology*, 67. Cf *Didachê*, IX, X & XIV.
3. Justin, *loc. cit.*

Testament and New, stories are told that belong to the 'family histories' of Israel and of Jesus' circle of disciples. We find many inspiring pages, but also tales of angry bloodletting and tearful lamentation, accounts of very public sin and of wrongdoing within the closer family circle. Today, as in early Christian times, the assembled local church listens to the inspired biblical word. Prophetic and apostolic pages are heard again, and understood in the light of Jesus' life and death. Worshippers express their response to this word, in psalm or canticle; then the teaching of Jesus is reiterated in gospel reading and commented upon in homiletic exhortation. Listening to New Testament texts, participants at the Eucharist eavesdrop on the excited atmosphere of discussions held among early Christians. But more than eavesdrop: those who attend to this word *belong* fundamentally to the very same community of faith that produced Acts, for instance, or Galatians or Matthew!

The homily seeks to turn eavesdropping on early disciples' attempts to understand Jesus' purpose into an exhortation to pilgrims to persevere along the pilgrim path (*cf* Heb 12:1f, quoted earlier). The homily can enable worshippers to receive afresh the Spirit who inspired the texts just heard. Gerhard Ebeling said the preacher's task here involves 'letting the text become God's word again'.[4] After the sermon, worshippers strengthen their faith in communal profession of belief, and are further unified as they list the intentions of prayer present in their hearts and minds as they come to church, as well as those emerging in the Eucharistic context of biblical reading and commentary.

III: WHEN YOU COME TOGETHER, 'DO THIS IN MEMORY OF ME'

Disciples are aware of the Lord's promise that 'the one who eats this bread will live forever' (Jo 6:58). The Saviour who said this is he who later opened the eyes of disciples on the road to Emmaus, explaining what was found in biblical scrolls. They would have known these texts, though they were as yet unaware of their immediate relevance. And although evening had drawn in and the disciples pressed the man they met on the road to stay overnight

4. G. Ebeling, *Word and Faith*, Philadelphia, Fortress, 1963, 329.

rather than remain on the road at that late hour, these very disciples are the ones who cannot now hesitate. Once it dawns on them just who this stranger is, they get up immediately and return to Jerusalem (cf Lk 24:33). They move toward another assembly, where the Eleven are gathered; the opening of their mind's eye in the breaking of bread leads immediately to their sensing a task ahead, a mission, as they await the fruit of the new vine in the 'kingdom', to be drunk by Christ himself and by those with him (cf Mt 26:29).

The definitive triumph of Jesus over sin is, in disciples' minds, fundamental to survival and flourishing. It was the Word of God made flesh who 'led captivity captive' (cf Eph 4:8; Ps 68:18), enabling his brothers and sisters to find the freedom of redemption, liberated now from the crippling imprisonment that was due to mismanagement of their inherent freedom. The Lord died, and this is central to the purpose of the liturgy; but the Word of God is also, and crucially, described as being 'alive and active' (Heb 4:12): the sacrifice of Calvary was not in vain.

The Bible recounts tales of exultant joy and acclamation for the Lord, but it also contains pages of darkness and of desolation in the human heart. The Liturgy of the Eucharist unifies contrasting themes: it stresses that both the 'Hosanna' acclamation as Jesus enters Jerusalem and the shouts of rejection/exclusion from the city apply to the very same person, for 'they have crucified the Lord of glory' (1 Cor 2:8). Those who gather in memory of Christ are called to offer themselves as a living sacrifice too, one that is 'holy and acceptable'; their minds are 'graced' in this sacrament so they can dare to go consciously where the obedient Christ went.

In the transformation – firstly of bread and wine, and consequently of all who partake of the sacrament – the Spirit of God is ever-present. Described in Genesis as being active at the very start, the Spirit is there too in the re-creation of the world by means of Christ's Passion. The Spirit who inspired biblical authors is the same who stirs believers, on hearing that sacred word, to live by it. After all, the biblical page has been opened for all disciples as it had once been 'unveiled' on the road to Emmaus. Furthermore, this Spirit motivates disciples' fidelity to Jesus and, in a sacramental moment, enables Communion with him that is truly profound. The

Spirit sends them out then, enthusiastic to nourish others with fruit provided them in the sacrament.

The liturgy, during which disciples are nourished first in Word and then in Flesh and Blood, is not an 'award-giving' banquet (or 'celebratory' in that sense); rather, it represents food for a journey as yet incomplete. This repast is repeatedly required by pilgrim athletes as they press on. Nor, while the history of salvation continues to unfold, can the biblical scroll ever be folded up and shelved. Its meaning has still to be further disclosed in the course of a pilgrim race as yet unfinished. It must be said also that for some the scroll has not even begun to be unfolded: multitudes of people have not as yet heard the good news.

IV: HE BEGAN TO PROCLAIM HOW MUCH JESUS HAD DONE (cf Mk 5:20)

The assembly of worshippers has sung, we may say, in unison; they have professed a united faith and received the One Bread and One Cup. This unity is a bond that links them also as they move out, going in all directions. Christ it is who binds them as one, wherever they may wander: 'get up and walk' (cf Jn 5:8) is an invitation addressed also to those disciples who have spent Mass-time in prayerful memorial of the Lord's Passion. The 'sending out' of the congregation comes with a reminder of the task ahead, to tell others what they have heard, tasted and believed. Disciples whose lives are enhanced by this sacred food can go and share its benefit with people who have never tasted the goodness of the Lord – and with some others who once walked closely in step with the Church but who have recently, for whatever reason, taken their distance. The Spirit will enable disciples to speak also to those who find it impossible to (re)join a worshipping community that has at some levels yet to appreciate how valid it is to speak of the Church as 'semper reformanda'.

As Matthew notes when the recounts the feeding of a multitude (15:32-39), the disciples were aware of the hungry crowd while being conscious also of the scarcity of food immediately available. Yet, in the Church's celebration of Jesus, as in the gospel text, nobody who participates need leave the gathering undernourished. 'I do not want to send them away hungry', says Jesus (v.32). The word of

Scripture, its proclamation, its explanation and the prayer it inspires, this is food for heart and mind. Eucharistic participation in the Lord's body and blood is a viaticum to sustain those who resume their missionary path after Mass. The Lord invited those who hunger to come to him: none of those who have been in Christ's presence ought to remain undernourished as they pursue the path their life is taking. Those fed at the Lord's Table are the ones called to go to the byways and invite further guests, so they too may belong. The good news must also reach those who today feel unforgiven and thus radically undernourished.

Nor is it without significance that Jesus' invitation in the last chapter of John, already quoted, called the disciples to 'come and have *breakfast*'. For when the service of worship is complete, a long day still lies ahead, time when these disciples are expected to do as instructed: 'tell ... what you have seen and heard' (*cf* Lk 7:22).

Without the Spirit's presence, the doors of places where disciples gather remain firmly shut (*cf* Jn 20:19ff). But when the Spirit comes upon the assembly (by means of a proclamation of the inspired word and a transformation of bread and wine into the Body and Blood of the 'beloved Son'), the Eleven and all disciples ever since can open the ears of heart and mind and 'Listen to him' (*cf* Mk 9:7).

PART ONE: ASSEMBLY

This essay forms the first part of an examination of links between Scripture and Eucharist. What follows now is an attempt to provide a brief introduction to the study of different stages of the Eucharistic celebration, treated in order. This will include an examination of the biblical background of the liturgy's major moments.

Gathering for worship, instruction and fellowship has been a constant feature of Christian practice. The Chosen People had traditionally come before the Lord too, and for specific occasions the assembly was in the Temple. The Eucharist is a congregation of a family united with Christ – it is gathered indeed by Christ himself – and thus can strengthen bonds of loyalty and love. The gathering itself is a kind of entrance antiphon: a common purpose is expressed by pilgrims who have assembled to refresh their memory of what

Christ did, to come again into an intimate Communion with him and then move on, a Spirit-inspired fresh vigour in their step.

When the family story is told in biblical word and elaborated in homiletic commentary, and when they 'eat this bread and drink this cup', the disciples enter into sacramental communion with the Lord they commemorate. In this manner the Body of Christ's disciples, a metabolism whose heartbeat is found in the union of the Lord's sisters and brothers, is strengthened further in prayerful worship and in a conscious sense of corporate mission.

PART TWO: CELEBRATING THE WORD

The Liturgy of the Word forges a chain to link the next seven chapters of this book, as our authors consider aspects of that part of Eucharist when the Word of God gathers us to hear the message again and gain fresh insight into how best it can be put into practice. Tom Brodie, in Chapter Two, notes the importance of seeing the Old and New Testaments as parts of one story: each part of the biblical story illuminates the other. Brodie highlights some features of the Old Testament without which, he notes, 'Christianity cannot flourish' (p 31). The first reading at Mass may come from either part of this story, but the Response (sung, ideally) is generally taken from the Book of Psalms. Mark O'Brien examines the place of the psalms in prayer. His essay (Chapter Three) does not shy away from difficulties posed by texts of psalms, including the question of lament, the issue of cursing, and the constant and often vexatious problems involving translation of these poems. O'Brien is certain the psalms provide opportunity and challenge for the translator, and he provides a range of examples.

Consideration of the psalms leads to a general examination of the question of music in the Eucharistic act of worship. Margaret Daly-Denton recounts how Jewish writings in the aftermath of the Temple's destruction in 70 CE frequently insist that 'to pray the psalms that formerly accompanied the sacrifices is as good – and even better – than offering sacrifices'. Our author notes, in this chapter, how rabbis taught that, since the absence of psalm singing would have invalidated a sacrifice, the real sacrifice was actually the prayer. Daly-Denton notes that in Greek and Roman philosophical works there are frequent instances where they question the whole idea of animal sacrifice, as a preamble to praising the practice of 'rational sacrifice', an inner worship by the human spirit. Jews, she notes, generally 'valued the singing of praise as a testimony to their devotion and gratitude' to God. Now, in our Eucharistic context, we know the congregation of worshippers yearn to become 'one body, one spirit, in Christ': the practice of singing psalms and hymns enables the community 'to sing and make melody to the Lord' (*cf* Eph 5:19; Ps 27:6).

The biblical reading heard just before the gospel is proclaimed can often come from Letters of St Paul or his circle – though other New Testament texts are used not infrequently, Revelation, say, or the 'Letter' to the Hebrews. It is worth reflecting, with Francis Moloney in Chapter Five, that some aspects of the mystery of Christ are found, among NT texts, only in the Pauline Letters. Thus, apart from the gospels, there are many 'summaries' of the mystery and significance of who Christ is, found in the Pauline texts; and this material provided valuable vocabulary for early Christian statements of faith. Paul's writings, as Moloney points out, insist that 'the sinful condition established by the sin of Adam has not disappeared', but also that 'grace and freedom' have been established in the new creation 'made possible in Jesus Christ'. This mystery of Christ is carried forward in the gospels too, and Donald Senior examines the role of these evangelical texts in the Eucharistic celebration. The fascinating three-stage formation process that led to the final redaction of the gospels is rehearsed again here (in Chapter Six), principally to point to the crucial part played by the Eucharistic gathering itself in the final editing of these texts. As some of that earliest group of witnesses to Jesus' life and teaching had now died, the stories being handed down and shared needed, in Luke's phrase, to be formed into 'an orderly account' (1:1-4). These sayings of Jesus and accounts of his deeds were told, proclaimed, and even gained their definitive written form, in the context and environment of Eucharistic celebration. There could be no clearer or more inspiring evidence than this of the link between the text of the gospel proclaimed and the homiletic reflection that follows it.

Preaching follows the gospel, and on this basis Jerome Murphy-O'Connor entitles his essay (Chapter Seven) *God's Priestly People: Preaching as Sacrifice.* St Paul admired especially Jesus' total dedication to his ministry: his life was a living sacrifice. The Apostle of the Gentiles considered the temple to be the place where God lived, and thus can speak to the disciples and say 'you are God's temple because God's spirit dwells in you' (1 Cor 3:16; 6:19). Murphy-O'Connor notes that since the 'fundamental activity of the temple... was sacrifice', it makes sense that Paul considered 'all aspects of the life of the Christian community in terms of sacrifice'. In a striking consideration of two Pauline verses (Romans15:15f), he links word and sacrifice. The preaching of the word in homiletic reflection on the biblical passages that have been proclaimed is seen in sacrificial terms, as is the offering of one's life ('a living sacrifice'), in imitation of Christ's complete dedication. Murphy-O'Connor notes also that we have evidence that the disciples in Corinth were fully aware of the (monetary) collection taken up – and the importance attached to it by Paul. It is a feature worshippers in all ages have been fully aware of. Although evidence of his practice is found in Paul – as Murphy-O'Connor mentions – and also in Justin, it is not a theme dealt with explicitly in our book. But when it comes to the collection, as Murphy-O'Connor notes, sacrifice is plainly to the forefront, whatever the cause and purpose of the collection.

Liam Walsh deals then in our eighth chapter with the Creed. Examining the development of statements/summaries of faith from the Old and New Testaments and then further into the early history of the Church, Walsh sees these creeds as, basically, statements of interpersonal relating in liturgical and doctrinal contexts, and he develops this reflection to take in the complex history of their development and use. Whether the context was immediately liturgical or (also) doctrinal, 'there was a need to get it right, to tell the truth about Jesus, about the God who is his Father, about the Spirit who is present and given in the interaction of Father and Son'. Walsh mentions a classical confession of faith among God's people (*cf* Deut 26:1-11), for it has some notable parallels in what takes place at the Eucharist. Once settled in the land given them by the Lord, the people of Israel are required to take 'some of the first of all the fruit of the ground', put it in a basket and present it in the place the Lord has chosen, acknowledging that they have come into the land the Lord had sworn would be theirs. The priest sets the basket of fruit down before the altar, and the one making the presentation pronounces a statement of faith, starting with an acknowledgement of family history ('A wandering Aramean was my ancestor…'). The worshipper recalls aloud some key moments of the people's story – told as family history. In the Church's Eucharistic assembly, the profession of faith leads presently to the bearing to the altar of the fruit of the earth and of human work: these will become not only symbols of the fruitfulness of land and labour and of people's gratitude for life but will be revealed as the body and blood of the Saviour, without whose presence the sacrament cannot be celebrated, tasted, believed.

PART THREE: CELEBRATING THE EUCHARIST

The Liturgy of the Eucharist is dealt with in the five chapters of Part III. This is the part of the Liturgy where the invitation issued by the Lamb of God to come to his Supper is heard again; and all who come are nourished. Thomas O'Loughlin examines the very structure of Christian prayer. There are Christological and Trinitarian prayers in our Missal, and other prayers of thankfulness. All of these are embedded in prayers recited during the Mass, in the first place in the Eucharistic prayer but also in the Collects and in the Prayer of the Faithful. This consideration of prayer in its many Eucharistic forms (Chapter Nine) may be considered a link between this book's examination of the Liturgy of the Word and the section beginning here, relating to the Liturgy of the Eucharist. The memory is recounted of the death and resurrection of Jesus, and in this context bread and wine are brought forward: the assembly prays that the Spirit will come upon them as the worshippers unite with Jesus in recalling the life-long prayer that was the Saviour's dedication 'unto death, death on a cross' (Phil 2:8). Daniel Harrington devotes Chapter Ten to aspects of Pneumatology: the Spirit in creation and in the remembrance of the Paschal mystery. Harrington examines *epiclêsis* and *anamnêsis* in the Bible and how vital this background is for understanding these terms in the Eucharistic context. Shortly after the Liturgy of the Eucharist has begun, there is the festive 'Holy, Holy!' acclamation. The very remembering of the Paschal Mystery makes present the hour of Christ's Glory.

Seán Freyne deals with this theme of Glory in the Old and New Testaments, recalling that the notion had a liturgical sense right from the start of its biblical treatment. 'The pre-eminence of the term glory (*kabod*) among the Hebrew epithets for God has given rise to the notion of the doxology as a central dimension of human recognition of the divine.' Freyne notes (in Chapter Eleven) how persuasively Hurtado argues 'that it was in the context of Christian worship that the first followers of Jesus began to ascribe divine status to him'. The Eucharistic Prayer concludes with an acclamation of assent, *Amen*, and the assembly then says or sings, together, the Lord's Prayer. A meditative reading of texts from Matthew, Luke and the *Didachê* is presented in Chapter Twelve by Leonard Doohan. In a sense, the Lord's Prayer is similar to a Creed in that it outlines, albeit in a text addressed to God, 'a summary of the key teachings that Jesus gave during his ministry'. These teachings, Doohan, points out, 'give us a picture of authentic discipleship'. The reality of this unity among disciples is the perfect moment for the Holy Communion that is about to take place. Séamus Tuohy then presents a striking reflection in Chapter Thirteen on the eschatological aspect of the Eucharist, linking Scriptural and Eucharistic features by means of the biblical-liturgical mention of an invitation to 'the Supper of the Lamb' (Rev 19:9). Worshippers partake of this supper, yet still await its definitive revelation. Disciples formed 'in the patience of God' can bear the impatience that attends expectation. As early as the *Didachê*, prayer at the end of the Eucharist included a final plea for *another* assembly:

> Gather her [the Church] from the four winds, separated into your Kingdom which you have made for her, because You have the power and glory for ever (*XIV*).

This 'already but not yet' aspect of this Supper involves the acknowledgement, just before Communion, of the unworthiness of those about to take it, to eat and drink. Any idolatry that might, in Tuohy's words, be 'inherent in arrogant self-sufficiency', is destroyed in the redemptive suffering of a humble servant. 'God's Messiah', Tuohy notes, 'conquers not as a devouring lion, but as a slaughtered lamb'. The triumph of the sacrificial victim has taken away the sins of the world. As the disciples celebrate and give thanks for a life that is renewed and redeemed, they 'come and take the flesh of Christ'.

PART FOUR: GOING FORTH

A disciple will need strength and courage in order to go forth confidently as a witness to what the Lord has done. In the closing rites of the Eucharistic liturgy, Christ reminds the assembled disciples (just nourished) that a task lies ahead. In the final section of this study, aspects of the life of disciples are examined: what their mission is once they are sent forth at the end of the liturgical assembly. Helen Doohan (Chapter Fourteen) sees St Paul as the archetypal apostle and missionary, and for us as for him the commemoration of Christ's sacrifice leads to being sent out, fortified by the nourishment of Word and Sacrament. In the dismissal of the worshippers, I hear also an echo of Moses' own report of the Lord's own words to the people: 'You have stayed long enough at this mountain. Resume your journey, and go to the hill country...' (Deut 1:6f).

Chapter Fifteen concludes our collection: Céline Mangan reflects on the presence of God, in every place, independently of any liturgical action. 'Nature is a temple', said Charles John Vaughan, quoted here by Mangan. The presence (of God) is no longer bound by Temple wall or precinct, but is also to be sought and located in all places the disciples go with the message they have learned and shared in the Eucharistic Liturgy. It is recalled that in Israel's ancient history, the exiles experienced 'a new and more profound understanding of God whose presence was not just to be experienced by them alone but by all peoples' (cf Isa 56:6-8). In the era during which Jesus lived, Mangan notes, Qumran covenanters took themselves off in protest, 'to await a new in-break of God's presence in a new Temple'. The Fourth Gospel (2:13-22, for instance) gives the clear impression that Jesus himself critiqued the Temple and its practices. He had come to inaugurate a new Temple, the Temple of his body, offered once and for all in the obedience of his utter dedication unto death (*cf* Heb 10:10; Jn 2:19-21). Let Mangan have the final word here: '... in trying to turn humankind back to a realization of the presence of God, Jesus had to experience in his own flesh the pain of that turning'. It is the pain of this New Covenant's inauguration, the dedication it involved, dedication that was to culminate in sacrifice, this is what is commemorated and gratefully celebrated in the Eucharist.

AD MULTOS ANNOS

This book seeks to treasure both biblical word and Eucharistic worship, researching so much that links them. But why now, and why in this manner? The answer is called Wilfrid Harrington.

The papers between these covers honour a participant in the pilgrimage we have spoken of. Wilfrid has constantly treasured the Sacred Scriptures of Old and New Covenants, and sought their meaning and purpose. In addition, he comes daily before the Lord, giving thanks for the nourishment of Word and Communion. But there is more. For Wilfrid is a runner in this pilgrim track who sees as his mission to instruct fellow disciples to love the Sacred Scriptures, and to nourish and encourage many who are not yet disciples or, for some reason, no longer run the race with the conviction of their younger days. The example of Wilfrid's transparent joy has meant for many disciples an injection of fresh hope: these then carry the treasure of word and sacrament further and share it with a wider circle.

His colleagues honour Wilfrid Harrington in this *Festschrift*, and record how much they value this colleague who has read the Word and spoken what he has learned. If there were a 'response' to each chapter that follows, perhaps it might be *Ad multos annos!*

Part Two

CELEBRATING THE WORD

Pantocrator

CHAPTER TWO

Why do Christians Read the Old Testament?[1]

THOMAS L. BRODIE OP

IN THE EYES of the famous New Testament expert Rudolf Bultmann, the Old Testament was a failure.[2] And many other Christians have had doubts about the usefulness of reading the Old Testament. It seems alien, at least compared to the apparent simplicity and familiarity of the New Testament. Yet the Hebrew Scriptures are the foundation of Judaism, a living faith with its own integrity. And a fellow countryman of Bultmann's warned: 'One who desires to think and feel in terms of the New Testament too quickly and too directly is in my opinion no Christian'.[3] Somehow the Christian needs the Old Testament.

But why? The full answer is beyond me, beyond the space of this article. One thing I know: I love the Old Testament. And to a significant degree that is due to Wilfrid Harrington who, when we were students in the 1960s, led us through the ancient scriptures with unflinching scholarship and generosity. What I will do here is simply highlight some Old Testament features without which Christianity cannot flourish.

---

1. The term 'Old Testament' is used here to designate the combination of the Hebrew Scriptures with the further books found in the Greek version of those scriptures, the Septuagint - the version most used by the New Testament writers and by early Christians.

2. *Scheitern*, 'failure, shipwreck, miscarriage', Rudolf Bultmann, *Glauben und Verstehen: Gesammelte Aufsätze II* Tübingen: Mohr Siebeck, 1952, 183.

3. Dietrich Bonhoeffer, quoted by R. E. Brown, 'Hermeneutics', in *Jerome Biblical Commentary* London: Chapman, 1968, 71:47.

AWARENESS OF HUMAN NATURE

John Moriarty was a gentle poetic-prophet from Kerry (once an imposing footballer!) and when he spoke in public, he would lift up his mighty hand, splaying the fingers, to show how close they are to ancient reptiles from which humans are descended. And not only reptiles but stars, for without the iron from exploding stars, human bodies could not be formed. In fact one of the oldest and most enduring ideas in philosophy is that the human being is a microcosm, 'a small epitome of the universe'.[4] So when on a given day a body is not feeling well, for some even obscure reason, it is appropriate to be considerate towards it: after all, given a body's complexity, heaven knows what is going on inside.

Heaven, and the Old Testament. The New Testament knows too, and may say so more vividly or with more insight. But the Old Testament spells out the detail of the drama, and often, rather than attempt to describe what is going on inside a person, rather than try to say the unsayable, it evokes it, and so comes nearer to giving a sense of it. This applies also to the struggle to stay with the truth, the tussle with sinfulness. Thus, the Old Testament, which often seems far from modern life and practical ministry, in fact can be very close to it.[5]

Human nature's complexity begins to emerge even as Genesis opens. Humans are described first as being in the image of God and then, while being in God's spirit, as made of clay. Despite the complexity of combining image-of-God with clay, the overall sense is of humans as good, in fact 'very good'. And the woman is integral to the 'very good' and to all the implied goodness of being one with the man (cf Genesis, chapters 1 & 2). This is a sharp contrast with a leading Greek account of what Zeus said in creating woman:

> ... I will give them an evil, and all men shall fondle,
> this, this evil, close to their hearts, and take delight in it.
> So spoke the father of all gods and mortals;
> and laughed out loud ...

4. Marilynne Robinson, *Absence of Mind* New Haven: Yale U. Press, 2010, xiii.
5. See, for instance, Denise Dombklowski Hopkins and Michael S. Koppel, *Grounded in the Living Word. The Old Testament and Pastoral Care Practices*, Grand Rapids, Mich.: Eerdmans, 2010.

but ... he gave instructions
to put in her the mind of a hussy,
and a treacherous nature (*Works and Days*, 59-68).

But when, to replace good,
He had made this beautiful evil,
He led her out ... this sheer deception ...
and hateful poverty they [women] will not share,
but only luxury.
As when inside the overarching hives,
the honeybees
feed their drones – and these are accomplished
in doing no good,
while the bees, all day long
until the sun goes down
do their daily hard work ... (*Theogony*, 585-597) .[6]

My sister calls this funny. It is also offensive, but it was written
by a prestigious Greek, Hesiod, a near contemporary of Homer
(around 700 BCE), and apparently was well known. It is important
to cite it, for two reasons. Firstly, like the frequent banality of evil
among cultured leaders, it shows the ease with which a seemingly
educated mind can slip into a mind-set that is grotesque. And
furthermore it almost certainly forms part of the background to
Genesis' account of the origin of woman.[7] But Genesis rebels against
it – as Genesis, despite its limitations, often rebels against other
aspects of ancient writing. Not only is the woman resoundingly
good, very good; she also shares equally the mission of men, and
in particular, in contrast to the drones, she shares the work. The
wording in Genesis, 'fitting helper' (Gen 2:20) has sometimes been
interpreted as demeaning, but against the background of Hesiod,

6. See *Hesiod. The Works and Days. Theogony. The Shield of Herakles*, tr. Richard
Lattimore, *Ann Arbor Paperbacks*, Ann Arbor, Mich.,University of Michigan, 1991.
7. Genesis absorbed and changed much of Mesopotamia's literature, it's long
been accepted; and evidence is now growing that the Hebrew writers also engaged
the world of the Mediterranean, including the Greeks. See especially the writings
of Cyrus Gordon, for instance, *Before the Bible: the Common Background of Greek and
Hebrew Civilizations*, London: Collins, 1962. For links to Homer and Hesiod, see T.
L. Brodie, *Genesis as Dialogue*, New York/Oxford: Oxford, 2001, esp.141, 447-494.

it is a declaration of dignity and responsible partnership. This does not prevent the Old Testament from being patriarchal, but it shows how the Old Testament challenged an earlier order, and it provided a precedent for further challenges. The Old Testament also reinforces the sense of woman's dignity and role by presenting several striking women, particularly Rebekkah,[8] and above all by personifying divine wisdom as a woman (especially in Proverbs 8, Sirach 24, and Wisdom 7:22-8:1).

Yet the OT has no illusions about human nature – men or women. Murder lurks. The New Testament simply *implies* the murderous streak. Simon/Peter swings a sword sufficiently close to someone's head to cut off an ear (Jn 18:10), and Saul/Paul was 'breathing ... murder' (Acts 9:1). But the Old Testament spells out a vivid drama: Cain, the first man born of natural parents, kills his brother; Moses, the peerless prophet who towers over the Hebrew Scriptures and Jewish tradition, begins his career by killing an Egyptian; and David, the engaging king whose narrative occupies far more space than that of any other ruler, arranges the death of his mistress's husband (2 Sam 11). And the Old Testament shows women as equally involved in evil. Jezebel arranges the death of a good man with just as much efficiency as David (1 Kings 21).

For anyone who oversimplifies people – and Christians sometimes do – the Old Testament dramas are a reminder to be more alert to deeper levels of both evil and goodness. And in these dramas the emphasis always falls, ultimately, on the conviction that regardless of the extent of evil, goodness is greater.

Few writings in any tradition dramatise the quest for goodness, for God, so evocatively as the Song of Songs. According to the great Rabbi Akiva (around 100 CE),

The whole world is not worth the day
on which the Song of Songs was given to Israel,
for all the writings are holy,
but the Song of Songs is the holiest of the holy.

8. Rebekkah's presence and actions have two levels, one familiar, even apparently unfair, the other close to the divine or to the woman involved in contention with the serpent: Brodie, *Genesis*, 2001, 280, 306.

In its elusive labyrinth the Song of Songs reaches through layers of desire to the place where the deepest desire in the human heart touches the heart of the divine. For this song alone it is worth having an Old Testament and wrestling with it.

AWARENESS OF THE PROGRESSION OF HUMAN LIFE

As well as giving some sense of the depth of human nature, the Old Testament also describes or evokes life's duration, its flow through the years. Obviously, many writings do this, most famously perhaps, at least in succinct form, Shakespeare's 'seven ages'. But the Old Testament seeks especially to get beneath the details. The story of Jacob has a complexity and detail that find nothing in the New Testament to match them: it is a tale that gives a person notice of what life is like. In an extraordinary brief meeting with Pharaoh, the aged Jacob describes the years of his life as 'few and hard' (Gen 47:9), yet in other ways his life is surrounded by blessing. He sometimes moans, especially at the loss of his beloved son, but generally he manages to see beyond such moaning.

Something of the same sense of the complexity of life is evoked in the great rambling drama that is the book of Isaiah. It is hardly an accident that Isaiah – whatever its complex origins – opens with an emphasis on children (Is 1-12), and that the later figure of the Suffering Servant (Is 42:1-9; 49:1-6; 50:4-11; 52:13-53:12) suggests a much older figure. For people who feel vaguely surprised and depressed by the progression of life, there is a message: Isaiah, a prophet of faith and hope, said there would be days like this.

AWARENESS OF GOD

Maintaining a sense of God is not easy. Hundreds of things distract, some gross, some refined – including disordered forms of preoccupation with religious organisation and study. 'Even ... exegetical research ... can become a sort of escape.'[9] Yet, no matter what the nature of the distraction, the desire for God remains, and

9. John Paul II, 'Address on the Interpretation of the Bible in the Church', 23 April 1993, paragraph 9, in *The Biblical Commission's Document "The Interpretation of the Bible in the Church", Text and Commentary*, Joseph A. Fitzmyer, *Subsidia Biblica 18*, Rome: Pontifical Biblical Institute, 1995, 6.

it would seem that two of the greatest revolutions to beset Christianity, those of Islam and Protestantism, were at root a quest for God, for a reassertion of God's sovereignty.

It may seem at first sight that Christians are unlikely to lose the sense of God. They, of all religions, have strongly asserted the closeness of God in the form of Jesus. Yet in 1975 Nils Dahl spoke about 'the neglected factor' in New Testament theology, and that factor was God.[10] Since then the neglect has been addressed, for instance by emphasising the role of God in John's portrayal of Jesus, or in trying to trace how Jesus came to be recognised as God.[11]

But these efforts to gain a sense of the God of Jesus have often been obscured by a preoccupation with reconstructing the historical Jesus, and the results have generally not been inspiring:

> The subjective role of the entire enterprise becomes evident: the framework chosen often reveals as much about the investigator as it does about Jesus. When scholars, all using the same methods and studying the same materials, derive such a variety of 'historical' Jesuses - a revolutionary zealot, a cynic radical, an agrarian reformer, a gay magician, a charismatic cult reformer, a peasant, a guru of oceanic bliss – then one may well wonder whether anything more than a sophisticated and elaborate form of projection has taken place.[12]

One of the results of this disproportionate emphasis on reconstructing the historical Jesus is that, insofar as Jesus is meant to communicate God, the confusion and restriction in the images of Jesus tends to generate confusion and restriction around God. In that sense, the historical Jesuses are becoming idols that distract from God.

10. Nils Dahl, "The Neglected Factor in New Testament Theology", *Reflections* [Yale Divinity School] 75 (1975) 5-8, republished in *Jesus the Christ. The Historical Origins of Christological Doctrine*, Donald H. Juel, ed. Minneapolis, Fortress, 1991, 153-163.

11. Marianne Meye Thompson, *The God of the Gospel of John*, Grand Rapids, Mich. Eerdmans, 2001; Larry W. Hurtado, *How on earth did Jesus become a god? Historical questions about earliest devotion to Jesus*, Grand Rapids, Mich.: Eerdmans, 2006.

12. Luke Timothy Johnson, *The Writings of the New Testament. An Interpretation.* Third Edition. London: SCM, 555.

This narrowing of the sense of Jesus seems to be part of a larger phenomenon in the western world, the narrowing whereby the Enlightenment turned out many lights except that of reason. Reason is wonderful, but alone it makes for a narrow world where not just Jesus but all people are reduced – for instance, in simplistic theses such as those of Freud or Dawkins – and where truth too is reduced, as if it could be expressed in tidy propositions.[13]

Meanwhile, the Old Testament still stands, a beacon of God's presence. At times that presence may seem negative, when God is angry, even genocidal. Certainly the ban on whole populations while conquering land (*eg*, Deut 2:34) is disturbing, and seems unintelligible in the context of God's general defence of innocent human life. Part of the explanation may lie in the ambiguity of the term 'land', which sometimes seems to refer not to a physical territory but to a realm of the spirit. Sue Boorer, for instance, argues on other grounds that

the 'land' itself must be symbolic of something more than simply a piece of territory ... Perhaps the experience of life with which these texts constantly struggle is akin to that captured in the words of T.S. Eliot,

In order to possess what you do not possess
you must go the way of dispossession... [14]

The banning of everyone encumbering the land may be kindred to the New Testament injunction that no one, not even family members, should encumber one's relationship to Jesus (and implicitly to God, Matt 10:37), to the example of the Buddha who left his family to follow the truth, and to Sartre's dictum that 'hell is other people'.

The essence of God's anger is that God takes wrongdoing seriously. There is no cover-up. In the opening account of creation, God seems distant, acting only through a commanding word. But as the goodness begins to unravel, God is less distant. When the

13. Robinson, *Absence of Mind*, 2010, especially 64-107.
14. Boorer, *The Promise of the Land as Oath: A Key to the Formation of the Pentateuch.* BZAW 205; Berlin/New York: De Gruyter, 1992, 449-450.

couple in the garden lose their way, God emerges as walking, the first character in the Bible to do so. Then God becomes closer, making strong clothes for the couple. When there is a murder, God intervenes, first on behalf of the victim, then to protect the perpetrator, effectively reaching out and touching him.

Later, when the whole world seems corrupt, God does indeed express ultimate anger by drowning it all, yet, in another sense, God is never so close, so involved. For the first time in the Bible there is a reference to a heart, the human heart which is so corrupt, followed in the next sentence by a further reference to a heart, that of God. In both sentences, the precise verbal formulation involving 'heart' is identical (Gen 6:5-6).

When the whole terrible drama of the deluge is over, when a human being, building on God's grace, makes a gesture towards God (Gen 6:8; 8:1,20), and when God realises that the human heart is even worse than previously stated – it not only contrives evil *all day* (Gen 6:5), but does so even *from youth* (Gen 8:21). For that very reason, God promises never to repeat the punishment, and, while protecting human life, God gives greater freedom in the choice of food. Thus, when the reason for condemnation is aggravated, the response is not greater condemnation but compassion. Long before devotion to the Sacred Heart of Jesus, the story of the Deluge provides a drama of the heart of God, ultimately drama of a forgiveness that surpasses human calculation.

The surpassing of calculation seems to be the best explanation for the contradictions in the numbers attached to the Deluge story. Petty calculation blocks forgiveness. It counts faults and wants to get even, to balance the books of war. But – like Jesus challenging Nicodemus and the Samaritan woman with apparent contradictions – Genesis challenges the reader to leave pettiness. It offers a wider space.

RESURRECTION

Jesus' resurrection is central to Christian faith, and often generates tense discussion. What exactly happened? The Old Testament helps the discussion because, just as Jesus himself comes somehow from within the Old Testament, so his resurrection also is part of a larger reality that illuminates the Old Testament. Even in Genesis 5, amid a litany of death ('Then he died ... Then he died ... Then he died...'), there is a strange variation: 'Enoch walked with God. Then he was not, for God took him' (Gen 5:24). The variation is so brief and isolated that it may seem insignificant.

Yet as the Primary Narrative unfolds – the great narrative from creation to Jerusalem's fall (Genesis to 2 Kings) – some episodes leave the reader asking 'What happened in that person's death?' Jacob's funeral (Gen 50) seems initially to fit within Egypt's lavish customs. But later, Joseph quietly asks that his father be buried at home. Then a few low-key verses describe the journey which, defying normal geography, has to cross the Jordan to reach the place that runs through Genesis like a haunting snatch of music – the cave in the field of Machphelah, opposite Mamre, which Abraham had bought as a burial site from Ephron the Hittite. Mamre, near Hebron, was the place where the ninety-nine year old Abraham had met God and showed a whole new level of life (Gen 18:1-15). And as 'the people of the earth/land' watch the great cavalcade on its way from Egypt to Hebron, all they see is what seems to be a great mourning of the Egyptians, and they have no idea that the journey to the cave in the field has a whole other meaning (Gen 50:4-14).

One is left guessing also by the deaths of others: Moses, buried apparently by God, but whose tomb, despite its well-known location, has never been found (Deut 34); the three people who, with increasing clarity, are raised from the dead by Elijah and Elisha (1 Kings 17:17-24; 2 Kings 4:8-37; 13:20-21); and above all Elijah who, like Enoch, effectively walked with God to his death, and like Moses could not be found (2 Kings 2:1-7, 16-18).

The Old Testament intimations of life after death reach a high point in Daniel 12 (note Wisdom 4:7-18; 2 Maccabees 7), but what is important is that Jesus' death is not an isolated event. It happened 'in accordance with the scriptures' (1 Cor 15:3-4) and that means that the resurrection is a much more complex reality than one isolated event.

CLUES TO THE NATURE OF THE NEW TESTAMENT

On Christmas Day 2010, Joe Duffy, an interviewer on Irish radio, asked some scholars about the Christmas story, and the prevailing response was that the gospels are essentially historical, and that this historicity has been strengthened in the last forty years. Apart from discussing Christmas, the programme touched a basic fact: despite all that has been written about the twenty-seven books of the New Testament, the nature of most of them is still not clear.

Initially their nature may seem obvious. The first five, the Gospels and Acts, consist of prose narrative, often like history-writing. And the remaining twenty-two are presented as Letters, often written with a letter's spontaneous emotion. However, it is clear that not all the letters are spontaneous compositions. The final letter, the Book of Revelation, while it 'is formally framed as a letter'[15] is in fact an apocalypse, a poetic account of a vision concerning God's presence and purpose in the world, and so is generally regarded not as a letter but as a multi-faceted apocalypse, a poetic vision. Likewise the letter to the Hebrews is generally regarded not as a spontaneous letter but as a carefully-crafted sermon.

The remaining twenty letter-like documents, thirteen bearing the name of Paul, are usually interpreted as spontaneous letters, though some researchers refer to some of them as epistles – something much more studied, a form of essay. Joseph Fitzmyer, for instance, speaks of Romans as a 'letter-essay'.[16]

So what are these letter-like documents? And what are the five history-like prose narratives? Some commentators do indeed see the debate as swinging in the last forty years towards greater closeness to factual history, and perhaps towards a greater sense of the historical role of Paul. And it is certainly true that, with the help of disciplines such as social science and archaeology, we now know far more than formerly about NT background, about the

15. David E. Aune, "Revelation, Book of", in *Eerdmans Dictionary of the Bible*, ed., David Noel Freedman, Grand Rapids, Mich.: Eerdmans, 2000, 1124-1127, esp. 1124.
16. Joseph A. Fitzmyer, *Romans*, Anchor Bible; New York/London: Doubleday, 1992, 90.

entire ancient world, including the places associated with Jesus and Paul.

But something else has happened in the last forty years, something that, compared to historical and sociological background, is closer to the question of the nature of the text. The New Testament is emerging as part of a larger literary world, and especially as coming out of the Old. The letters bearing Paul's name are being recognised as carefully reflecting OT narrative, and the extent of this dependence on OT narrative is still not clear. In the words of Bishop N. T. Wright of Durham:

> Once the narrative genie has been let out of the bottle, not least in a world with its eyes newly opened by contemporary literary study, you can't get it back in; and now all kinds of aspects of Paul are being tested for implicit and explicit storylines.[17]

What is true of the Pauline writings is increasingly true of all the Letters, and true also of the five prose narratives. In varying ways the NT writings are emerging, despite all their genuine newness, as carrying the literary genes of the older scriptures.

This is a massive topic, still largely undeveloped. Yet already it is worth noting. Christians cannot continue to read the New Testament without taking account of the nature of the underlying Old Testament writings. And these writings, while embedded in history, as is Christianity, make enormous use not of hard facts but of stories and poetry.[18] The methods of composing Hebrew narrative apply to the New Testament also, to a degree yet to be determined.[19] In the case of the Book of Revelation and the Letter to the Hebrews, the pervasive dependence on the OT is clear. It remains to be seen whether such dependence is exceptional, or whether it is the tip of an iceberg.

17. N.T. Wright, *Paul: in Fresh Persepctive*. Minneapolis, Minn.: Fortress, 2005, 7.
18. See, for instance, David J. A. Clines, "Story and Poem. The Old Testament as Literature and as Scripture", *Interpretation* 34 (1980) 115-127.
19. Such methods are outlined, for instance, in Robert Alter, *The Art of Hebrew Narrative*, New York: Basic Books, 1981.

THE NEED FOR DIALOGUE AND PROPHECY

The OT has a remarkable way of showing diverse aspects of reality. Its two accounts of creation, far from being unrelated, are a delicate balance of opposites: humans created in the image of God, but also made of clay; created to rule the earth, but also (in the second account) to till it, literally, to serve it; married to procreate children, but also for companionship. Genesis maintains an ideal of marriage, just two people. The book is framed by the unions of the first parents, and of Joseph and his wife. But while guarding that ideal, Genesis seems to find it necessary or wise to acknowledge that stuff happens in human lives, and so it portrays two foundational characters, Abraham and Jacob – the father of faith and the father of the nation respectively – as living with complex marriage situations. Even Moses' marriage is questioned (Num 12). Likewise regarding government: kingship is enabling, but it can also be oppressive (1 Sam 8). In fact the structure of entire books seems to be based on various forms of dialogue or dialectic.

A further form of dialectic comes from the prophets. Prophecy can probably be described as the foundation of the entire Old Testament. The Pentateuch, for all its complexity, is attributed essentially to Moses, who was regarded above all as a prophet. The subsequent narratives also (Joshua to 2 Kings) were known traditionally as prophetic ('the Former Prophets'), and even when the time of the great prophets (Isaiah, Jeremiah, and so on) has passed, their heritage continues to be revered – for instance in Ezra, who is like another Moses, in Daniel, and in Sirach which at the culmination of its central chapter declares,

All this is no other than the book of the covenant of the Most High God, the Law that Moses enjoined on us (Sir 24:23).

Prophets were foundational insofar as it was their insight and vision that could see, on the one hand, the depth of the evil around them, and yet on the other could show people a way forward, a path to meaning and peace. Prophets of course were often troublesome. Moses troubled the most powerful man in the world, and the later prophets often troubled everybody. But essentially prophecy founded the Old Testament and offered hope.

The situation among Christians is more complex. Christianity is now spread widely, and Catholicism in particular is a huge institution. Institutions can bring great benefits, whether in disaster relief, or in organising education, health care, different forms of service, or a broad vision for a positive life, plus the supports to attain it. But organisations, in their laudable desire to be effective, very often leave little room for dialogue or prophecy. Earlier it seemed easier. Paul had no qualms about confronting Cephas/Peter (Gal 2:11-14). But once western Christianity split, Christians entered into a kind of permanent Cold War, and in war there is little room for divergence of view or for prophecy. Some of the Cold Wars are now over – much of the edge has gone off both the East-West rupture and the Catholic-Protestant divide, but just as that is happening other divisions are opening up – bitter antagonisms within countries or within churches. And so once again, there is little room to express difference or to propose a further vision. In this situation the spirit of Old Testament prophecy is sorely needed.

CHAPTER THREE

The Psalms in Translation

MARK A. O'BRIEN OP

W HEN WILFRID HARRINGTON published his *Record* trilogy[1] in 1965-66, the Second Vatican Council was drawing to a close and the wider church was implementing the vernacular in the liturgy after nearly 2,000 years of Latin. Less than a decade earlier, the French Dominican school, the École Biblique, had completed *La Bible de Jérusalem* translation, and in 1966 an English version, *The Jerusalem Bible* (JB), was published and was adopted as the text for the Lectionary.[2] The JB joined a growing collection of English Bibles; many were the work of biblical societies in the Reformed tradition but the new ecumenical spirit led to a number of these being issued as 'ecumenical editions' for use by a wider public than the members of a particular church.[3] Providing translations of biblical and liturgical texts became a thriving industry and continues to be so, as indicated by two recent major projects: the new English translation of the Missal and the École Biblique's BEST proposal – a new translation of the Bible with accompanying notes.[4]

The aim of this essay is to explore and assess some of the factors driving the modern Bible translation industry. The Psalter provides a suitable focus for such a task, both in relation to translators and

1. *cf* Bibliography of Wilfrid J. Harrington, p 199 below.

2. *La Bible de Jérusalem* Paris: Cerf, 1956; *The Jerusalem Bible* London: Darton, Longman and Todd; New York: Doubleday, 1966.

3. For Catholics, ecumenical editions meant that Books were included from the larger Catholic canon (the deutero-canonical books) that are not part of the Reformed canon (which adopted the shorter Hebrew list of inspired books).

4. The term is an acronym for *La Bible En Ses Traditions*, in English 'The Bible in its Traditions'. The project was launched in 2006 and contributions can be accessed at www.bibest.org.

their readers. The psalms are poems, and poetry is customarily regarded as a more 'elevated' form of discourse about things that matter; this tends to heighten the challenge for translators and the expectation of readers. [5] Psalms are recited or sung as part of the daily *Prayer of the Church* and as responses to Lectionary readings. They are also used widely for private prayer. One can assume therefore that, as Old Testament texts go, they are fairly familiar. They also provide some contact with other perhaps less familiar parts of the Old Testament by referring or alluding to themes and issues in the Pentateuch or Torah, Prophetic and Wisdom Literature. Despite this, they do not all fit neatly into mainstream Roman Catholic worship and piety. Many are classified as lament psalms, and laments are not a significant feature of our liturgies. Others are classified as cursing psalms and tend to be excluded from public recitation. The curse at the end of the otherwise popular Psalm 137 is a classic example. Overall, one could say that the psalms provide opportunity and challenge for a translator, leading to comfort or discomfort for a reader. There is an Italian saying that states that the translator is a 'traitor' (*Traduttore, traditore*).

Bible translation is of course not a recent practice. Nehemiah 8 may well be the earliest written record of Hebrew being rendered in a language familiar to listeners/readers, in this case those who had returned from the Babylonian exile in the late 6th century BCE and who no longer knew Hebrew. The translation was most likely into Aramaic, the lingua franca of the ancient Near East. A similar situation in Alexandria in the 3rd century BCE resulted in a Greek translation (the Septuagint – LXX). We sometimes speak of translating from the Hebrew 'original' but there is no original text of the Old Testament available. It is generally agreed that the Hebrew behind the LXX differed in varying degrees from the one

5. A basic feature of Hebrew poetry is parallelism, in which the second line normally resumes and develops the preceding one. The first line of Psalm 24:1 is 'The Lord's is the earth and its fullness', with the second 'the world and all its peoples' (Grail). Parallelism can sometimes express a contrast (cf. Psalm 1:6), or involve more than two lines. Robert Alter's recent translation strives to reproduce Hebrew parallelism as closely as possible, even to comparing the number of syllables per line of the English to that of the Hebrew (*The Book of Psalms. A Translation with Commentary* New York/London: W. W. Norton and Company, 2007, xxx-xxxi).

that became the standard text for later Judaism (the Masoretic Text or MT). The Dead Sea scrolls reveal evidence of other Hebrew 'originals'. Does this say something about human limitations and/ or something about the nature of the Word of God? That is, it can be expressed in human words but not captured or contained by any one version of them – another way of saying that the Word of God is living and active, ever old and ever new. Difference or variety is evident within the Bible itself: a clear example is the at times quite different accounts of Israel in the Former Prophets (or 'the Historical Books') and the Books of Chronicles.

In terms of theory, Bible translation through the ages has oscillated between literal and more liberal/flexible approaches, what some call a source oriented and a target oriented approach. Each claims to present an authentic version of the text to the reader or receiver. A literal translation stays as close as possible to forms and conventions of the source language whereas a flexible one seeks to incarnate its meaning in the target language of the receiver – entering its forms and conventions. The LXX is regarded as a literal translation of the Hebrew in comparison to the Aramaic Targums, but this was not good enough for the subsequent Greek versions of Aquila and Theodotion. They are even more literal than the LXX. In the Latin-speaking world, Jerome saw his Vulgate translation as an authentic rendering of the Hebrew original (he had studied the language) but Augustine and others were critical.[6]

As one might expect, modern Bible translation theory and practice reflects to a considerable degree major developments in modern Bible study, and the study of literature in general. Until recently the dominant one has been historical critical or diachronic analysis that seeks to discover how biblical texts came about; from their origins to what is called their final redaction (editing). This has tended to favour a more literal translation in so far as practitioners endeavour to identify as accurately as possible the original text and the circumstances of its production (the author, the culture, the time, etc). More recently however, philosophical and literary theory has shifted attention to the dynamics involved

---

6. See 'Jerome's Vulgate' in Roland H. Worth Jr., *Bible Translations. A History Through Source Documents* (Jefferson, North Carolina, & London: McFarland & Company, 1992) 27-41.

in the act of reading a text (synchronic analysis). According to this view, readers do not simply receive the meaning of a text but create it anew in each act of reading – as evidenced by different readings. Critical (responsible) readers must of course respect the parameters established by an author, otherwise they cannot claim that their reading is authentic. One may say that, once a text has been composed, its author becomes its reader along with other readers, albeit a rather well informed one. This approach tends to favour a more flexible or creative translation. Some examples may help to illustrate the difference between the two approaches.

Mitchell Dahood's three-volume commentary on the psalms, the first volume being published in the same year as Harrington's *Record of Revelation*, exemplifies the drive to recover the original version that characterises historical critical analysis, in particular form criticism.[7] A good example is his translation of Psalm 63:3 (63:4 in the MT) – 'How much sweeter your kindness/than my life and lips that praise you'. In contrast, the popular Grail version used in the English Breviary has – 'For your love is better than life/my lips will speak your praise'. Dahood appeals to Ugaritic, a language 'whose closest affinity is to biblical Hebrew',[8] to help recover the original sense of the psalms. He proposes that the Hebrew term normally translated as 'good/better' should be rendered 'sweet/sweeter', based on Ugaritic and parallels in Psalms 33:3; 45:2. He also proposes that the MT of v. 3 needs to be corrected to preserve a Hebrew grammatical rule that 'After subjects of different genders, the predicate is put in the masculine plural'.[9] The subjects are 'life' (masculine) and 'lips' (feminine) and the predicate is 'praise you'. The correction involves shifting the final letter from the preceding word (life) to the following word (lips). The result is a double comparison 'than my life, than my lips' rather than the single as in the Grail translation. This is possible because Hebrew words were not separated in early manuscripts and mistakes were no doubt made during the later separation process. However, the notion of 'my life' praising God does not occur

7. Mitchell Dahood, *Psalms I, 1–50; Psalms II, 51—100; Psalms III, 101–150* Anchor Bible, New York: Doubleday, 1965, 1968, 1970).

8. Dahood, *Psalms I*, xix.

9. Dahood, *Psalms II*, 98. It is recognised however that Hebrew poetry, like other poetry, does not always obey the rules.

anywhere else, nor does the combination of 'my life' and 'my lips' praising God. The difference between the two translations is theologically significant. In Dahood's version three sweet things are compared, God's (your) kindness and my life and my lips, with the first being sweeter than the others. While the contrast between the possessive pronouns 'your' and 'my' is effective, my preference is for the Grail translation which – following the MT – draws a dramatic contrast between two things, God's love and life itself. The psalmist can do no other than praise God's love, the good on which all others, such as life, depend.

Historical critical analysis also endeavours to retrieve the original meaning of texts by comparing ancient manuscripts. For example, the MT of Psalm 8:2-3 (8:1-2 in English) is unclear and Greek, Syriac and Aramaic (Targums) manuscripts offer variant readings. Depending on which reading one adopts a different translation emerges with a different understanding of the role of infants in the text. Two of these are reflected in the RSV and the NRSV revision:

Thou whose glory above the heavens is chanted
by the mouths of babes and infants,
thou hast founded a bulwark because of thy foe
to still the enemy and the avenger (RSV).

You have set your glory above the heavens.
Out of the mouths of babes and infants
you have founded a bulwark because of your foes,
to silence the enemy and the avenger (NRSV).[10]

In the RSV, the role of infants is to sing of God's glory; in the NRSV their voices serve as a bulwark against God's foes, reducing them to silence. Should one adjudicate between these translations and understandings – each can claim to be as authentic or original as the other – or accept two differing and powerful images of the role of infants in God's scheme of things?

The form critical quest for the original text claimed to uncover a phenomenon that has come to be of central importance for historical

10. Barbara Pitkin, 'Psalm 8:1-2,' *Interpretation* 55 (April 2001) 177-80.

critical analysis, and is relevant for the theory and practice of translation. It is called redaction, the editing of texts to update and apply them to new situations. The pursuit of the original version meant that terminology and expressions that did not appear, from a critical point of view, to fit the recovered original were deemed to be later additions. These were initially regarded as relatively unimportant, theologically, but in time redaction criticism has assumed increasing importance. Redactors are now seen as skilful theologians who carefully reworked existing texts to give them new life and meaning. Differences between manuscripts are now also seen, at least in part, as evidence of this interpretative process.

Antony F. Campbell argues that Psalm 78 was originally composed as a theological interpretation of events leading up to the establishment of the Davidic monarchy.[11] It claimed that they signalled God's rejection of the rebellious Israel of Shiloh and the election of David's Jerusalem. The original was subsequently edited by deuteronomic theologians to apply its teaching to their accounts of later reforming kings, most likely Hezekiah or Josiah. Campbell identifies deuteronomic additions in vv. 5-8, 10, 56b, 58. The nature and strategic location of these additions suggest that the editors or redactors carefully studied the original version of the psalm as well as the situation(s) to which they applied it. They saw that the original conveyed a message they could apply creatively – but still authentically – to a new situation, a new audience.

An interesting aspect of the redaction of biblical texts is that it has something in common with the more flexible side of the translation equation. Both share a focus on the reader or receiver. Nevertheless, translation is a more complicated process than the inner biblical process of editing/redaction. Two languages and their respective authors or readers are involved, as well as the translator who also functions as a reader in relation to the source language. As noted earlier, more recent biblical exegesis has shifted attention from the relationship between author and text to that between reader and text. Their relationship has been explored not only by biblical scholars but also by translation theorists, a major figure in the biblical arena being Eugene A. Nida. A member of the Methodist

---

11. Antony F. Campbell, S.J., 'Psalm 78: A Contribution to the Theology of Tenth Century Israel,' *Catholic Biblical Quarterly* 41.1 (1979) 51-79.

Church and an active missionary as well as an academic, Nida has spent a lifetime seeking to provide a translation that is accurate yet enables the Bible to speak in the target or receptor language in a way that ordinary people can understand.[12] This involves paying attention to the context of both the source language (the biblical text) and the target language. One must study not only the philology and grammar of each language but their sociological, cultural and religious contexts as well. Translation is an interdisciplinary matter.

The scope of biblical translation also led Nida to be one of the earliest Bible translators to employ discourse analysis in addition to philology and grammar. Communication is always a structured affair, and discourse analysis examines how words, phrases and sentences are combined or structured to produce whole texts such as a Psalm or a Book. In effect, Nida and his team doubled the historical critical agenda. They applied their critical tools not only to the source language but also to the target one. Their goal was 'that the relationship between receptor and message should be substantially the same as that which existed between the original receptors and the message'.[13]

Yet historical critical analysis has come to realise that it is difficult to be certain how people in biblical times responded to texts. Some prophetic texts report people's reactions, particularly to negative prophecies, but the psalms provide little information about how people responded to them and used them. Some superscriptions or titles provide clues (Psalms 120-134, for instance), each of which is entitled *A Song of Ascents*. They may have formed a prayer book for those making the pilgrimage 'up' to Jerusalem. But, was this their original setting and use? Lack of certainty on this side of the translation equation is compensated for to an extent on the other side of the equation – the response of those in the receptor language: this *can* be measured. But even here Nida came to see that a translator's observations could only go so far. To be sure that a translation makes sense to native speakers (the subjects) of the target language, a translator needs to listen and learn from them.

12. Eugene A. Nida and Charles R. Taber, *The Theory and Practice of Translation*, Leiden, Brill, 1969

13. Nida, *Toward a Science of Translating: With Special Reference to Principles and Procedures Involved in Bible Translating* Leiden: Brill, 1964, 159.

Nida described his translation theory and practice as dynamic equivalence, to distinguish it from the more literal approach, what was called 'formal' equivalence. Later, in the light of criticism and reflection, he altered the description to 'functional' equivalence. The best-known example is the Good News Bible (GNB, 1976). Its translation of a key verse in the famous 'miserere' Psalm 51, namely v. 5 (v. 7 in the MT) invites some comment and comparison: 'I have been evil from the time I was born/from the day of my birth I have been sinful'. There is quite a difference between this and the more literal (and familiar) rendering in the RSV: 'Behold, I was brought forth in iniquity/and in sin did my mother conceive me' (cf the NRSV; 'Indeed I was born guilty/a sinner when my mother conceived me'). The RSV is closest to the Hebrew (which is also followed by Dahood) and one suspects that the GNB and the NRSV are seeking to make sense of this text to an English language readership that a) is individualistic and b) would object to the implication that conceiving a child is (always) a sinful act. Both translations focus on individual sin and either eliminate reference to the mother (GNB) or transfer the reference to sin from her to the psalmist (NRSV). While these translations catch the pervasive presence of sin in one's life, they fail to capture other features of Hebrew thinking about sin – such as the connection between individual and community, between past and present, as well as a sense of the general state of human sinfulness. Hebrew has a variety of terms for sin: their meaning and relationship is fluid and depends to a considerable degree on context. Without going into the details, I would suggest that the parallel statements in v. 5 refer to the general state of human sinfulness that touches life at all stages, from the begetting of it to the living of it. One may also note that the GNB translation gives the impression that the psalmist committed sins from the day of birth. This would presumably strike a modern English reader as strange and perhaps even as offensive.

This is one example from a translation that has proved popular and helpful to many in the English-speaking world. Critics from the literal or formal equivalence side have found plenty of other examples to object to, and a vigorous debate has developed between the two approaches. Y. C. Whang, for instance, argues that the variety of readers and contexts in the receptor or target language makes functional equivalence untenable. The translator's job 'is to convey the idea of the author, and to understand the idea is the role of the reader'.[14] Stephen Prickett objects that dynamic or functional equivalence's desire to make sense of the Bible in a target language risks obliterating the subtlety and ambiguity of the original, particularly in poetic discourse.[15] Simon Crisp notes that in the Orthodox tradition the biblical text is likened to an icon that provides only limited access to the mysterious world of the all holy.[16] Phyllis Bird believes that a translation should allow a modern audience 'to overhear an ancient conversation rather than to hear itself addressed directly'.[17] While these are telling comments, advocates of functional equivalence can reply that they do not take into account sufficiently the biblical conviction that God does speak to readers and listeners directly and in a very human way, as indicated by the second person singular and plural address in Deuteronomy, the lively language of Prophetic discourse, and the report in Acts 2:8-11 that all those listening to Peter's Pentecost sermon – the Word of God according to the biblical claim – heard it in their own language. As the Acts text in particular makes clear, God speaks in all the languages of human beings: one could say that there is no sacred language or that all are sacred because the Word of God is able to be incarnate in all. This is different to Islam where Arabic is regarded as the one sacred language. But the more literal camp could reply by saying that, according to Christian belief, God became incarnate in human form in order to transform humanity. Therefore, shouldn't one faithfully transmit those strange and mysterious biblical texts in the belief that they will transform the target language, rather than take charge by having the biblical text conform to the target language?

14. Y.C.Whang, 'To Whom Is a Translator Responsible—Reader or Author?' in Stanley E. Porter and Richard S. Hess, *Translating the Bible. Problems and Prospects* JSNTSup 173; Sheffield: Sheffield Academic Press, 1999, 46-62; *cf* 55.

15. Stephen Prickett *Words and the Word. Language, poetics and biblical interpretation* Cambridge: CUP, 1986, 31-32.

16. Simon Crisp, 'Icon of the Ineffable? An Orthodox View of Language and Its Implications for Bible Translation,' in A Brenner and J W van Henten, eds., *Bible Translation on the Threshold of the Twenty-First Century. Authority, Reception, Culture and Religion* JSOTSup 353; Sheffield: Sheffield Academic Press, 2002, 36-49; *cf* 42.

17. Quoted in Philip C. Stine, *Let the Words be Written. The Lasting Influence of Eugene A. Nida* Atlanta: SBL, 2004, 163.

The debate goes on. One may ask if there is any way of resolving the differences between the two. Susan Bassnett and André Lefevere judge that the notion of some universally valid way of translating is no longer viable, if it ever was, particularly in the modern arena: 'specific translators decide on the specific degree of equivalence they can realistically aim for in a specific text'.[18] If this is a fair comment about the general situation in Bible translation, the recent Roman document *Liturgiam Authenticam* indicates that the Vatican is moving firmly in the other direction. To gain approval from a Bishop's conference or the Holy See, translations will need, a) to show literal and not functional/dynamic equivalence, and b) contain minimal 'horizontal inclusive language' and avoid altogether 'vertical inclusive language' (in relation to God).[19] These requirements differ considerably from the ones enunciated at the Vatican Council in the instruction *Comme le prevoit* and which guided the work of ICEL and its 1994 translation of the Psalter.[20] According to a recent article by Emil A.Wecla a key factor driving the recent changes is inclusive language.[21] One can understand the desire for a standard biblical text for the church's public liturgy and, given the church's long use of the Vulgate, a more literal translation policy is hardly surprising. But it is doubtful whether this will replace the wide variety of translations now available to the English speaking public. The variety of translations both past and present alerts us to the limitations of our ability to translate the Bible; it signals the limitations of the biblical text itself in expressing the Word of God, as Jn 21:25 makes clear; it also schools us to listen and learn from these various translations.

18. Bassnett and Lefevere, *Translation, History and Culture* London: Continuum, 1998, 2

19. *Liturgiam Authenticam*: *Fifth Instruction on Vernacular Translation of the Roman Liturgy* Washington, DC: United States Conference of Catholic Bishops, 2001

20. See 'Instruction *Comme le prevoit* on the translation of liturgical texts for celebration with a congregation, 25 January 1969', in International Commission on English in the Liturgy, *Documents on the Liturgy 1963-1979* Collegeville, MN: Liturgical Press, 1982, sec. 841. Readers may like to compare these with the BEST translation guidelines in 'The Bible in Its Traditions: Definition of a Scientific Project' at www.bibest.op

21. Emil A.Wecla, 'What Is Catholic about a Catholic Translation of the Bible,' *Catholic Biblical Quarterly* 71.2 (2009) 247-63.

CHAPTER FOUR

When in our Music God is Glorified

MARGARET DALY-DENTON

When in our music, God is glorified,
and adoration leaves no room for pride,
it is as though the whole creation cried:
Alleluia!

How often, making music, we have found
a new dimension in the world of sound,
as worship moved us to a more profound
Alleluia!

So has the Church in liturgy and song,
in faith and love, through centuries of wrong,
borne witness to the truth in every tongue:
Alleluia!

And did not Jesus sing a psalm that night
when utmost evil strove against the Light?
Then let us sing, for whom he won the fight:
Alleluia!

Let every instrument be tuned for praise!
Let all rejoice who have a voice to raise!
And may God give us faith to sing always:
Alleluia![1]

---

1. © 1972 Stainer and Bell.

THIS HYMN by Methodist minister and poet Fred Pratt Green (1903-2000) is often chosen for occasions when the role of music in our worship is highlighted and celebrated: St Cecilia's Day, for instance, the dedication of a church organ, or the institution of new choir members. Set to Charles Villiers Stanford's stirring tune, *Engleberg*, it never fails to inspire. The authenticity of its account of the experience of making melody to the Lord (*cf* Ps 27:6) has been recognised by the many Christian communities all over the English-speaking world who have included it in their hymnals. This essay takes the form of reflections on the role of music in the Eucharist prompted by lines in this hymn.

WHEN IN OUR MUSIC, GOD IS GLORIFIED

The *Didachê*, written in the late first century CE, includes this instruction on the Sunday Eucharist: 'Having assembled together on the day of the Lord, break bread and give thanks, having first confessed your sins, so that your sacrifice may be pure.'[2] It is important not to read into this exhortation much later understandings of the Eucharist as a sacrifice. Clearly what this first-century Church leader has in mind is the community's giving of thanks as a 'sacrifice of praise', in other words, the singing that is not only better than sacrifice but is the real sacrifice that true worshippers offer to God, provided, of course, that their way of life corresponds to what they sing. When the *Didachê* urges that this sacrifice should be pure, the author is almost certainly thinking of a verse from Malachi that crops up frequently in early Christian writings about the Eucharist: 'For from the rising of the sun to its setting, my name is great among the nations, and in every place incense is offered to my name, and a pure offering, for my name is great among the nations, says the Lord of Hosts' (Mal 1:11).[3] To understand this early Jewish Christian reference to sacrifice in this way is to hear in it the echoes of a well-documented biblical

---

2. *Didachê* XIV.1.
3. *e.g.* Tertullian, *Against Marcion* III, 22. IV, 1; Irenaeus, *Against the Heresies* IV, 17, 5-6.

teaching: true sacrifice is not the offering of animals or produce, but the devotion with which they are offered to God. We find this insight expressed in the psalms, for example, where it is assumed that God regards the lifting up of the worshipper's hands in prayer as an evening offering of incense (Ps 141:2) or where joyful singing of praise is clearly as acceptable to God as any sacrifice (Ps 27:6).

The idea of spiritual sacrifice comes through strongly in the Dead Sea Scrolls. These are believed to have been produced by a community of ascetics established in the 1st century BCE and still in existence at the time of Jesus. This sectarian group withdrew in protest from what they saw as the corrupt Temple cult in Jerusalem and went into the desert to form an alternative 'spiritual temple'. In the hymn that concludes their *Community Rule*, for example, the leader declares, 'I will bless [God] with the offering of that which proceeds from my lips (1QS X, 13-15), alluding to a prophetic passage frequently invoked in the scrolls as biblical authorisation for the community's notion of spiritual sacrifice: 'Take away all guilt; accept that which is good, and we will offer the fruit of our lips' (Hos 14:3). When an early Christian leader writes – also alluding to Hosea – 'Through [Jesus] then let us continually offer up a sacrifice of praise to God, that is, the fruit of lips that acknowledge his name' (Heb 13:15), he is showing his awareness of this kind of thinking.

It is worth looking at this spiritualised view of sacrifice against the background of Greco-Roman religious developments, which would most certainly have been an influence, particularly in the Diaspora and the more Hellenized urban centres in Israel. Among Greek and Roman philosophers there had long been serious questioning of the whole business of animal sacrifices to gods. These thinkers believed that 'rational sacrifice', an inner worship by the human spirit, was much more worthy of the gods than sacrificing animals. This thinking encouraged forms of worship that emphasised hymn-singing. The infiltration of Greco-Roman religion by the Egyptian Isis and Serapis cults, where hymnody played an important part, would also have been influential. Some philosophers, including Philo, even went so far as to say that singing was a lower form of worship compared with the mind's wordless contemplation of the divine.[4] And yet the Jews generally valued the singing of praise as bearing testimony to their devotion and gratitude to their God.

LET ALL REJOICE WHO HAVE A VOICE TO RAISE!

When the author of the *Didachê* wrote, his people, including those who had become believers in Jesus, were still reeling from the blow of the Temple's destruction in 70 CE. Jewish writings from the aftermath of the trauma frequently insist that to pray the psalms that formerly accompanied the sacrifices is as good – even better – than offering sacrifices; and this is the belief of religious Jews to this day. The early rabbis even taught that since the absence of psalm singing would have invalidated a sacrifice, the real sacrifice was actually the prayer. In this they were helping people to cope with a new reality – the loss of the sacrificial cult, the means by which Israelites could maintain and repair their relationship with God. But this was not a new teaching. The rabbis were drawing out the implications of a deep conviction that had been gaining ground over centuries: that true sacrifice is the joyful praise sung to God.

Reference to the Eucharist as 'a sacrifice of praise' is a constant feature of the Christian euchological tradition. If singing our hearts out in our celebration of the Eucharist is to be an authentic expression of dedication to God, our way of life has to correspond to what is expressed in our song. For the early Christians, Jesus was the perfect example of this correspondence. And that is one way of understanding how the early believers came to see that the death to which he went with the psalms on his lips (Mk 14:26, 15:34; Lk 23:46) was indeed the perfect sacrifice. Authenticity also requires the active participation of 'all who have a voice to raise' in the church's singing. It is not at all impossible that Paul had precisely this in mind when he appealed to his brothers and sisters, 'to present [their] bodies as a living sacrifice, holy and acceptable to God' and that this would be their spiritual, literally their 'reasonable (Greek: *logikê*, rational) worship' (Rom 12:1), that is, their 'sacrifice of praise'.

4. Everett Ferguson, "Spiritual Sacrifice in Early Christianity and its Environment", in *Aufstieg und Niedergang der Römischen Welt*, II Principat 23.2, ed. Wolfgang Haase, Berlin & New York: De Gruyter, 1980, 1151-87.

IT IS AS THOUGH THE WHOLE CREATION CRIED: ALLELUIA!

Anyone who has received singing lessons from a good teacher will remember the thrill of their first really well produced note and of the extent to which this was a 'whole body' experience. For most people, learning to sing entails discovering that one should be involving far more of oneself than one's mouth; it requires learning to engage one's whole being: from the heels right up through the abdomen and the entire respiratory system to the top of the head. Real singing is a special way of breathing, a deep drawing in and a letting go of the air on which we depend for our very life. Breathing is a powerful symbol of life, a process that we share with the whole of nature. In biblical thought, our very existence depends on God breathing air into our nostrils (Gen 2:7; 7:22). Conversely, when God takes that breath away, living things die (Ps 104:29); the ultimate danger is water rising to our neck (Hebrew: *nephes*, breath), the critical site for our ability to breathe (Ps 69:1). According to the final verse of the Psalter, everything that breathes has its own way of emitting an *alleluia*. Human beings, though, are the only living things in creation that can channel their breath with loving intentionality into vocal praise of their creator. And in doing so they become enthused (Greek, *en theos*, in God); they breathe God in; they are inspired by God. Singing is thus the perfect expression of that giving of oneself to God, a giving that becomes reciprocal because we receive so much more than we give.

AS WORSHIP MOVED US TO A MORE PROFOUND *ALLELUIA!*

Music has that special power, associated with all art, to capture our attention and draw us into surrender. When we allow its beauty to affect us, 'normal' time is somehow suspended and we enter a different world. If we can yield to this, we may find unbidden memories, regrets, and buried longings surfacing as we become more and more lost in thought. At first, these seem to be a distraction, a deficiency in our concentration, but they may well be the gift that the music is giving us. Music can indeed seep through those defences that shield us from the pain of acknowledging our hurt or our incompleteness. But then it can also exhilarate us, freeing us from the restraints that inhibit our capacity to be celebrants of life. At these moments, music fills us with a sense of wholeness, of aliveness and, especially if we experience it with others, commonality.

When this kind of thing happens in the context of worship, music can become a way into prayer, opening us up to the transforming presence of God. It is often within the Christian community at liturgy that we find ourselves able to allow music to reach what is censored deep within us. Sometimes, but not always, this may happen because the music is the bearer of that word that 'discerns the thoughts and intents of the heart' (Heb 4:12). Often it is more a case of the beauty of the music itself luring us into being 'vulnerable to the Holy', to use an expression of Enda McDonagh's.[5] Saint Augustine seems to be thinking of something like this when he writes of the role that music played in his conversion: 'I wept at the beauty of your hymns and canticles and was powerfully moved at the sweet sound of your church's singing. Those sounds flowed into my ears and the truth flowed into my heart: so that my feeling of devotion overflowed and the tears ran from my eyes and I was happy in them'.[6] When music touches us deeply like this, there is potential for a purifying of the heart that is full of promise for a new seeing of God. Equally, it is especially in the context of 'a sacrifice of praise' that music can catch us up into a surge of adoration that lifts us beyond ourselves to the Other and out of our individualism into communion with our fellow worshippers. It is not by chance that biblical theophanies are so often described in musical terms (Isa 6:3-4; Lk 2:13-14; Rev 4:8).

SO HAS THE CHURCH IN LITURGY AND SONG …
BORNE WITNESS TO THE TRUTH

For Augustine, the verbal content of Church music seems to have been as much a factor in his experience as the beauty of the music itself. An awareness of the power of music to enhance the communication of the word and to impress it on memory and emotions

---

5. The title of an essay in which he meditates on the poetry of Gerard Manley Hopkins: Enda McDonagh, Vulnerable to the Holy: in *Faith, Morality and Art*, Dublin: Columba, 2004, 138-147.

6. *Confessions* IX, vi, 14.

is evident in the whole history of Christian ritual song which is, by and large, a history of the 'performance' of the Bible. The solemn public reading of Scripture has traditionally been performed in chant or cantillation: music and the Bible belong together.

The most detailed New Testament description of singing is found in Colossians 3:16: 'Let the word of Christ dwell in you richly; teach and admonish one another in all wisdom; and with gratitude in your hearts sing psalms, hymns, and spiritual songs to God'. In the first century CE there was considerable fluidity with regard to terminology, so it is difficult to know how exactly a hymn might have differed from a spiritual song. Even the designation 'psalm' was not restricted to the 150 canonical psalms. Jewish authors regularly referred to the psalms as hymns, especially when writing for a non-Jewish readership.[7] In the original Greek, Colossians 3:16 is a single sentence. The NRSV (cited above) breaks the sentence up into more manageable units, but unfortunately this gives a false impression of three consecutive actions: hearing the word of Christ, then a teaching session, followed by some singing. A more literal translation would read as follows – 'Let the word of Christ dwell richly in you [who are] in all wisdom teaching and instructing each other, [while you are] singing psalms, hymns and spiritual songs with thankfulness in your hearts to God'. In this reading, ritual song emerges as one of the ways Christians teach each other to hear the risen Christ speaking in the community. The New Testament evidence for the Christian reception of the psalms would suggest that frequently, when the early believers listened to what was sung – whether a biblical psalm or a new composition in psalm-style – they would have heard it as the 'voice' of Jesus.[8]

In what appears to be a re-working of the Colossians passage, the author of Ephesians suggests that worshippers who address one another in their psalms and hymns and spiritual songs are 'singing and making melody to the Lord' (Eph 5:19, alluding to Ps 27:6). The context indicates that 'the Lord' to whom this psalm/

---

7. Josephus, for example, refers to the psalms as 'songs and hymns' (Ant. VII, 305). For Philo, King David, supposed author of the psalms, is the hymnist (Greek: *hymnesas*) of God (*Conf.* 149).

8. Lk 24:44; Mk 15:34; Rom 15:3; Heb 10:5-7.

hymn singing was being addressed is, in fact, 'the Lord Jesus'. Maybe singing like this was what Pliny the Younger had in mind when he wrote around 112 CE in his report to the Emperor Trajan on this new Christian sect, '[They claim that] the sum of their guilt or error is to assemble on a set day before dawn, to sing among themselves a hymn (Latin: *carmen*, a song) to Christ as to a god and to commit themselves to an ethical way of life' (Ep. X, 96).

All of this points to the role of music in the Church's 'witness to the truth'. The traces of liturgical song in the New Testament are our earliest sources for Christian doctrine: the Christ hymn in Philippians, the Prologue to the Fourth Gospel, the short creed in 1 Tim 3:16, to mention just a few. On the principle that the law of prayer establishes the law of belief, it is clear that if we want to get back to the sources of our Christian faith, we should look at what the earliest Christians were singing![9] We know, for example, that they regularly sang, 'Taste and see that the Lord is good' (Ps 34:8) as they partook of the Eucharist.[10] As Greek speakers, their version of the psalm was 'Taste and see that *chrêstos* [is] the Lord'. The word *chrêstos*, (usually translated 'good') looks and sounds very similar to the word *Christos*, Christ (anointed one, Hebrew: *Messiah*) which became a kind of proper name for Jesus. The fact that in some early biblical manuscripts the two words are confused ('italicism' – a common scribal error) confirms that they were pronounced in a similar way.[11] Moreover, *Chrêstos* – with its range of meanings including 'useful', 'propitious', 'nice' – was a common proper name, especially for slaves.[12] So when an early Christian leader reminded his audience of their first initiatory sharing in the Eucharist when they sang, 'Taste and see that *chrêstos* [is] the Lord' (1 Pet 2:3), we cannot escape the impression that these worshippers,

9. The dictum of Prosper of Aquitaine († c. 450), *ut legem credendi lex statuat supplicandi* (that the law of prayer may establish the law of belief) is often cited in the form, *lex orandi, lex credendi* (the law of prayer [is] the law of belief).

10. *Apostolic Constitutions* VIII, 13, 1 (2nd to 3rd century). In his *Commentary on Isaiah* 1, II (4th century), Jerome also refers to the communicants' singing of Ps 34:8a every time they are satisfied with the heavenly bread.

11. *Christos* appears in 1 Pet 2:3 in several ancient manuscripts, the earliest being the fragmentary 3rd to 4th century papyrus P72.

12. See Paul's pun on *achrêstos*, 'useless' and *euchrêstos*, 'useful' in Philemon 11.

who received the Scriptures aurally, would have thought they were singing, 'Taste and see that Christ is Lord'. In this way they would have learned from what they were singing that it was through sharing the Eucharist that believers were enabled to believe and profess that 'Jesus Christ is Lord' (*cf* 1 Cor 12:3).

AND DID NOT JESUS SING A PSALM THAT NIGHT?

The evangelist Mark has bequeathed to us the gift of that precious little temporal clause, 'when they had sung a hymn' (14:26). In view of the fluidity of terminology mentioned above, and also because Mark envisages the Last Supper as a Passover meal, we can fairly confidently identify this 'hymn' as all or part of the 'Egyptian Hallel' (Psalms 113-118, traditionally associated with Passover). Singing at table was not restricted to this annual festival, however. The gospel accounts of Jesus' meals – Luke's descriptions in particular – show undisputable traces of the conventional Hellenistic meal: a supper followed by the symposium, which was a time for the sharing of wine, musical entertainment, perhaps an address by a guest of honour, poet, sage or philosopher, and general debate. Sources contemporaneous with the gospels indicate that psalmody was a Jewish 'substitute' for the paeans sung to the gods at pagan *symposia*.[13]

The delightful image of Jesus singing with his disciples at table can be supplemented with what we know of pilgrimage customs. Groups of pilgrims sang en route to Jerusalem: 'You shall have a song as in the night when a holy festival is kept; and gladness of heart, as when one sets out to the sound of the flute to go to the mountain of the Lord, to the Rock of Israel' (Isa 30:29). When we read in the gospel about Jesus 'going up' to Jerusalem, we should imagine him with the group who travelled with him from Galilee, leading 'a throng' – about one hundred and twenty of them, according to Luke (Acts 1:15) – 'in procession to the house of God with glad shouts and thanksgiving, a multitude keeping festival' (*cf* Ps 42:4). And then there is the noisy singing at Jesus' final

13. In the *Testament of Job*, a retelling of the biblical Job's story, dated around the turn of the era, Job claims that he regularly sang psalms with his lyre for the widows – twelve tables of them! – having entertained them to a meal (TJob 10:2; 14:1-5).

pilgrimage, with even the children daring to raise their voices in the temple (Mt 21:15-16), a commotion that provoked the reproof, 'Teacher, order your disciples to stop!' to which Jesus replies, 'If these were silent, the stones would shout out!' (Lk 19:39-40).

LET EVERY INSTRUMENT BE TUNED FOR PRAISE

One of the most exciting musical sounds is that created by the tuning of the instruments and the frenetic last ditch repetition of technically challenging passages before an orchestral performance begins. This is the fifty-ninth minute of the 'eleventh hour', as it were, the end of a lengthy process that began with the composer's work and continued through the performers' interpretation and rehearsal. It is only because all this work has been done that the improvisatory flash of inspiration, that makes a live performance unique, can occur. The calligrapher Denis Brown draws a helpful analogy between the process of making music and the careful pre-planning and rough work that goes into a piece of aesthetically pleasing script: 'As in most music, calligraphy for me involves a composing stage first, and practice after that to be able to make a final performance which is not a mere copy of the "score" but a lively rendition where random happenings in each stroke cause improvisation in the next'. [14]

Similarly, someone gifted with ability to read the Scriptures effectively in the liturgy will have spent time studying the passage and practising the reading aloud to the point where it is all but memorized, deciding exactly where to put the emphasis, where to change register, at what point to increase the pace or slow down. Yet in the actual liturgical 'performance' a new insight may be given, inspiring the reader to speak a word or phrase quite differently to what was intended. The hearer of the word too, who perhaps is familiar with the passage or has even intentionally studied it beforehand, can be surprised by a 'revelation' that is the gift of that particular 'performance' on that particular liturgical occasion. Setting the Scriptures to music requires similar attention to

14. *The Edge* (Journal of CLAS, The Calligraphy and Lettering Arts Society), 16.3 (2010) 4.

interpretation and rehearsal. The composer needs first to seek understanding of the passage through study, and then to speak it aloud, over and over, allowing the interpretive inflections and emphases that naturally occur to suggest melodic contours and rhythmic patterns. There is a sense in which the resulting musical composition is no more than a suggestion as to how a biblical passage might be read. The full task of opening up the text's revelatory potential is passed to the performer and ultimately to the listener. In the context of Christian worship, the performer is a minister, the listener is a worshipper. Often both are one and the same: 'the performing audience'.[15]

The contemporary British composer Francis Pott wrote in a letter to the dean of a cathedral where he had heard his liturgical music being performed, 'It is a strange sensation to find one's artistic efforts "staring back" at one, somehow no longer one's own, but proclaiming one merely the vessel or conduit for something given from elsewhere'. Liturgical music can have an effect out of all proportion to the capacities of its composers and performers. For believers, that 'lively rendition' of the Scriptures in song is ultimately the gift of the Spirit. The singing of the Easter Vigil gospel comes to mind. It was set to a simple chant consisting mainly of monotone, with only the slightest of inflections to point up the dramatic moments of the narrative and with an understated organ accompaniment of sustained chords creating a barely perceptible aura around the text. For one worshipper, kind enough to share his reaction, the experience of this modest musical setting of the gospel text was like 'hearing the good news of the resurrection for the first time'.

> How often, making music, we have found
> a new dimension in the world of sound,
> as worship moved us to a more profound
> *Alleluia!*

15. The title of a seminal collection of essays by the Dutch liturgist and church music composer Bernard M. Huijbers and published by North American Liturgy Resources, Cincinnati, 1972.

CHAPTER FIVE

New Testament Letters: Why Read them Still?

FRANCIS J. MOLONEY SDB

THE LETTERS of the New Testament are the Cinderella of the post-Conciliar Lectionary, and it is right that we ask why we read them. The Liturgy of the Word in the post-Conciliar Lectionary attempts to construct a thematic unity between random Old Testament passages and a continuous reading of Gospel texts. This leads to the appearance of the letters of the New Testament as an *intermezzo* between a perceived thematic unity of the Old Testament reading and the Gospel.

It is a matter of concern that the letters of the New Testament have long stood at the heart of the liturgical practices of our Protestant brothers and sisters, but play a secondary role in the Catholic preaching tradition. I am privileged to dedicate the reflection that follows to Wilfrid Harrington OP, a figure whose concern for the integrity of the Word of God in the life of the Church and for all believers has been an inspiration to generations of scholars and believers of all Christian traditions. Thank you, Wilfrid: *ad multos annos*.

THE PLACE OF THE LETTERS IN THE LECTIONARY

The Pauline readings across the ordinary Sundays of the year are gathered in brief sequences, scattered across the three years of the Sunday Lectionary. There is never a cursive reading of the whole of any one letter.[1] The Sunday Lectionary is made up of an even

---

1. For the allocation of the letters within the Lectionary, see a handy list in Frank J. Matera, *Strategies for Preaching Paul* (Collegeville: Liturgical Press, 2001), 184-86.

spread of readings from Pauline and non-Pauline letters, with about half of the readings coming from authentic Pauline writings.[2]

The greater part of 1 Corinthians is read across the three years. Four of Paul's shorter letters are read in different years: 1 Thessalonians (Year A), Galatians (C), Philippians (A), and Philemon (C). Paul's greatest letter, to the Romans, is only read in Year A. The non-Pauline readings come from Colossians, Ephesians, 1-2 Timothy, Titus, 2 Thessalonians, and Hebrews.

Frank J. Matera has wisely written: 'Once preachers have familiarised themselves with the letter's historical and literary contexts, they are ready to interpret the texts they will preach'.[3] The location of the letters, and their piecemeal selection renders this practice difficult. Nevertheless, we continue to read them. Why? Who was Paul? Why do we call some letters non-Pauline? How important are they? What was Paul's contribution to the beginnings of Christianity? Some responses to these questions will help us understand why we read the letters of the New Testament.[4]

PAUL AT THE BEGINNINGS OF CHRISTIANITY

Paul was the first person to begin a tradition of writing about Jesus. On three occasions the Acts of the Apostles tell of a remarkable conversion experience he had while on a journey to Damascus (Acts 9:1-30; 22:3-21; 26:9-23). Paul insists that he has been overcome and transformed by 'the power of the resurrection' (Phil 3:10). Prior to that experience, however, the idea that Jesus of Nazareth could have been the Christ would have been discounted by Saul of Tarsus. After all, he had been hung upon a tree, and this had already been described in the Old Testament as a curse (Deut 21:23; see Gal 3:13). The message was also abroad that Jesus had been raised from the dead. What these Christians were claiming for a man who had been crucified as a criminal was a stumbling

---

2. On the meaning of 'non-Pauline', see below.

3. Matera, *Strategies*, 9. This deceptively modest book is a valuable resource for anyone who wishes to focus upon the Pauline readings in preaching.

4. What follows develops Francis J. Moloney, *A Friendly Guide to the New Testament* Melbourne: John Garratt Publications, 2010, 12-13, 16-21, 53-58.

block for any Jew (1 Cor 1:23). Saul wanted to ensure that such teaching should not take root and corrupt any of his fellow-Jews.

Some might be tempted to believe that the scandal of the cross had been overcome by God by means of a resurrection. A thousand years of Israelite religious history and Paul's formation as a Pharisee were threatened by this new movement. He joined the opposition to the new-fangled religion based on a message that the man who had been crucified by the Romans had been raised, and was in some way 'alive' among those who believed in him and tried to follow his teaching. Paul's passion for the God of Israel could not tolerate this betrayal. Yet something happened to Saul of Tarsus that transformed him into the greatest of the early Apostles. Paul did not have a 'conversion' as we understand that word. His passion for the God of Israel always drove him; he now found that God made known in the crucified and risen Jesus of Nazareth. But he never lost his love for his people and their God (see Romans 9-11).

Paul does not tell us 'the story' about the birth, life and teaching of Jesus. From the letters of Paul, we know that he was 'born of a woman, born under the law' (Gal 4:4). In writing to the Corinthians, Paul reminds them that the night before Jesus died he celebrated a meal with his disciples that transformed Jewish Passover practices. He was giving his body and his blood to form a new covenant. They were to give their own bodies and shed their own blood in memory of him. Every time they were to do this, they would be proclaiming Jesus until such time as he came back again (see 1 Cor 11:17-34). Throughout his letters Paul focuses upon the obedience of Jesus, supremely manifested in Jesus' death. But if the obedience of Jesus led to crucifixion, the response of God was his raising of his Son from death (see 1 Cor 15:1-8). Paul's scant reference to Jesus' birth (Gal 4:4), his final meal (1 Cor 11:17-34) and his death and resurrection (1 Cor 15:1-8) play into his message of the obedient Jesus crucified and risen. We are at the heart of the Pauline gospel.

WHY READ THE 'NON-PAULINE' LETTERS?

We regularly hear the name "Paul" associated with 2 Thessalonians, Colossians, Ephesians, Titus, 1 and 2 Timothy, and the Letter to the Hebrews. About half of the Lectionary readings from the letters of the New Testament come from this collection. There are good reasons for suspecting that Paul was not the author of all these letters.[5]

Both 1 and 2 Thessalonians deal with the problem of the end of the world, and the attitude believers must have as they wait for that time to come. But 2 Thess 2:1-12 claims that there are some who believe the day of the Lord has already come, and the author responds to this by a description of that time. We do not find this anywhere else in Paul. The author seems to go out of his way to insist that he is 'Paul'. He insists on his authority on a couple of occasions (see 1:1; 3:14-15,17), unlike his other letters. It seems that he protests too much, and this arouses suspicion. Most likely 2 Thessalonians is an 'imitation' of the authentically Pauline 1 Thessalonians, but addressing a later situation.

Colossians develops a rich theology of creation, and God's saving presence in Jesus Christ, the high point and perfection of all creation. In Colossians 2:8-23 the author opposes a 'philosophy of empty deceit', the result of 'human tradition' and the 'elemental spirits of the universe' (v. 8). The author seems to be dealing with a false way of understanding the world that puts Christ in a position lower than some system of elemental spirits in a way that seems foreign to the world addressed by Paul. Only Christ is the universal and cosmic redeemer. This understanding of Jesus Christ does not change from Paul's fundamental point of view. It is being transported into a later time and place. Although the situation has changed, the Pauline tradition that no human system responds to the design of God for the salvation of humankind remains firm. The author can point to the uselessness of Jewish ceremonial law, taboos, and calendar observances (see 2:16-18, 20-22). Only one thing matters: 'holding fast to the Head, from whom the whole body, nourished and knit together through its joints and ligaments, grows with a growth that is from God' (2:19). The importance of oneness in Christ is found throughout the Pauline letters (see, for example, Rom 6:5-11), but Paul never quite says it like this.

---

5. It is unfortunate that, despite almost two hundred years of careful scholarship, the Lectionary still attributes these letters to Paul.

Ephesians also seems to reflect a time later than Paul and possibly depends upon Colossians. The author develops a magnificent theology of the unity of the Church. The hostility between Jew and Greek has ended because of Jesus' death. It is not as if this subject is non-Pauline. Indeed, it is a clear continuation of Paul's understanding of the significance of Jesus' death (see Rom 15:5-6). However, he has never before approached this subject in this way. Both Colossians and Ephesians begin to show a concern for the right order of the Christian household (see Col 3:18-4:1; Eph 5:21-6:9). Paul's never-failing insistence on love (see especially 1 Cor 13:1-13) is behind these more practical recommendations.

The letters to Titus, 1 and 2 Timothy, also claim to come from Paul. They are written at a time when the Churches addressed by these documents are well-established communities, beginning to feel the strain that always emerges as a developing group must cope with its human frailty. How leaders are to behave, how elders, widows and slaves are to be treated, how to distinguish between heresy and right teaching, are important issues that did not overly bother Paul during his career. These documents, generally well described as the 'Pastoral Epistles', probably date from the end of the first century, or early in the second century. Paul had been dead for some forty years, but his message still had to be passed on to a new and different generation of Christians.

Claiming that Paul was the author of a letter when he was long since dead may appear dishonest to us. But in antiquity it was quite common to use the name of a significant figure from the past as the author of a document, especially when that figure remained the inspiration for the author. These letters that look back to Paul for their authority are an example of a widespread practice in antiquity, known as 'pseudonymity'. We must be careful not to apply our criteria of today to judge this widely used practice. Whoever the authors were, they made the Pauline understanding of God, Christ, the Christian, and the community of the Christian Church their own. They do not betray Paul; they have taken Paul's message to heart. They apply it to later times and situations.

Tensions within different groups in the community were felt; problems concerning correct or false interpretation and teaching of what God had done in Jesus, and how they were to live as a consequence of that, were emerging.

Paul's authentic letters were written to specific groups in the earliest Church (remember Paul had been martyred by the mid-sixties). He did not have to face the internal and external problems that Christians faced later in the first century. The letters Paul certainly wrote are 1 Thessalonians (written from Corinth about 50 CE), Galatians, 1 Corinthians, 2 Corinthians, Philemon, Philippians (all written during a long stay in Ephesus from 54-57 CE) and Romans (written from Corinth in 58 CE). Inspired by that heritage, the later letters claim the authority of Paul by their steady reference to him as 'author'. He is their author in so far as he is their *authority*.

The Letter to the Hebrews does not claim to be Pauline. Subtly and with elegance it argues that all God's former institutions and means of communication with humankind have been perfected in Jesus Christ. The new covenant was foreshadowed in the Law of Moses and came to reality only in the person and work of Jesus. Hebrews has a unique literary form, is a superb sample of Greek writing, and was certainly not from the pen of Paul, and dates, probably, from the last decade of the first century.

This summary presentation of the non-Pauline letters suggests why we continue to read them. Paul's heritage was neither forgotten nor neglected. The early Church faced different times and circumstances with the Pauline letters in hand. In order to continue Paul's voice, they used his authority to speak his message in different words to different times. This task remains with us today, as we face our different times and circumstances with the Pauline letters and the Pauline tradition as our sure guide.

WHY READ THE PAULINE LETTERS?

The beginnings of an answer can be found by first reflecting upon the impact that the death and resurrection of Jesus made upon Paul, and his passion to communicate that through his unforgettable letters. Unable to review all that Paul wrote, we will reflect upon two critical texts, where his message is expressed with power and elegance: Phil 2:5-11 and Rom 5:12-21.

THE POWER OF THE RESURRECTION

Paul was a Jew 'of the people of Israel, of the tribe of Benjamin, a Hebrew born of Hebrews'. He also tells us in this text that he belonged to the Jewish sect of the Pharisees (Phil 3:5). Paul was transformed by what we might nowadays call a 'religious experience' that turned his life around to such an extent that he spent his whole life, even to the point of martyrdom, in a passionate gift of himself to preaching the gospel: 'Woe to me if I do not preach the gospel' (1 Cor 9:16). Paul's original passion for God was not changed by means of a conversion. He experienced a 'call' from that God to recognise and proclaim what God had done for humankind in and through his Son.

> But whatever gain I had, I counted as loss for the sake of Christ. Indeed I count everything as loss because of the surpassing worth of knowing Christ Jesus my Lord. For his sake I have suffered the loss of all things, and count them as refuse, in order that I may gain Christ and be found in him, not having a righteousness of my own based on law, but that which is through faith in Christ, the righteousness from God that depends on faith; that I may know him and *the power of his resurrection*, and may share his sufferings, becoming like him in his death, that if possible I may attain the resurrection from the dead (Phil 3:7-11. See also 1 Cor 1:18; 2 Cor 4:7; 12:9; 13:4).

The source for Paul's relentless and passionate conviction that these are the only things that matter is *the power of the resurrection*. At the heart of his preaching was Jesus' death and resurrection.

> For Jews demand signs and Greeks seek wisdom, but we preach Christ crucified, a stumbling block to Jews and folly to Gentiles, but to those who are called, both Jews and Greeks, Christ the power of God and the wisdom of God. For the foolishness of God is wiser than men, and the weakness of God is stronger than men (1 Cor 1:22-25).

Crucifixion is transformed into power and wisdom, weakness into strength. Jesus' death and resurrection make sense of our nonsense, and draw us into a 'new creation'.

THE DEATH AND RESURRECTION OF JESUS: PHILIPPIANS 2:5-11

It appears that there was division among the Philippians. Immediately prior to the hymn he writes: 'Do nothing from selfish ambition or conceit, but in humility regard others as better than yourselves. Let each of you look not to your own interests, but to the interests of others' (vv. 4-5). The Philippians knew the hymn that now follows. But by telling them 'Let the same mind be in you that was in Christ Jesus' (v. 5), he warns that the hymn they recite may tell Christ's story, but does not tell the story of the Philippians. He asks them to put their lives where their words are.

This famous hymn unfolds in four stages. The first is brief, describing Jesus' pre-existent divine state. But it affirms that Jesus did not cling on rapaciously to the honour of being equal to God. The rare Greek noun used, *harpagmos*, may indicate 'something to be grasped after'. It is well chosen here, for we tend to cling jealously, to grasp and hold firm to our honours. The point is that this is precisely what Jesus did *not* do: though was 'in the form of God', 'he did not regard equality with God as something to be exploited' (v. 6). Paul speaks directly to the Philippians, and through the letter to us all. As we seek honours and glory in our achievements, Christ Jesus did exactly the opposite. He lets go of his oneness with God. His status was divine and he let it go; our status is fragile and sinful, but we 'grasp onto it jealously'.

This leads the hymn into the first step in the second stage – the first description of Christ's humiliation. Jesus does not simply 'let go' … he 'empties himself' of all such dignity to take on the situation of a servant and slave. He comes into the history of frail human beings as a frail human being: he became as men are. But the second description of Jesus' humiliation points out that he lowered himself in human eyes to the lowest of the low, he accepted the cruelest and most humiliating death – death on a cross. Only when Jesus gives his unconditional 'yes' to God on the cross is his humiliation complete. This is the most perfect form of unconditional *obedience* that one could ever expect from a human being.

The hymn has had a downward swing from the pre-existent Christ, equal to God, to a human being, who was also a crucified slave. The unconditional obedience of Jesus has touched the human story in a 'once and for all' fashion, and this has its consequence. Jesus' unconditional 'yes' to God is now met by an unconditional 'yes' from God. Because of what Jesus did out of obedience to God and for all of us, he is raised on high by God. The theme of the hymn begins its upward swing with this turning point in the unfolding hymn: in the resurrection God has highly exalted him. Through the resurrection, the Christ returns to the place he abandoned so that we may have life and hope.

The result of God's exaltation of his Son does not lead the Christ to a distant place on the altars on high. Jesus' death and resurrection have changed the nature of the relationship between God and humankind. He is given the name of Lord. All creation recognizes what he has done and bends the knee in recognition of the saving act of God that has taken place through obedience unto death and the exaltation that takes place in resurrection. Jesus Christ is now our Lord and the Lord of all. We no longer have to wait for the end of all time for the establishment of God's 'right order'.

We confess that Jesus Christ is Lord; we recognize the glory of God … but only if we are prepared to accept Paul's initial invitation to 'walk as Jesus walked': 'Let the same mind be in you that was in Christ Jesus'. The story of Jesus must be repeated in the story of all who claim to follow him. In this way our lives will be caught up into the rhythm, scope and ultimate victory of the same divine plan.

THE NEW CREATION: ROMANS 5:12-21

On two occasions, Paul speaks (without explanation) of the death and resurrection having generated a 'new creation' (Gal 6:15; 2 Cor 5:17). He does not use the expression elsewhere, but Paul's understanding of what God has done for us in the death and resurrection of Jesus is a 'new creation'. We looked at Phil 2:5-11 for a concise outline of Paul's central message on Jesus' death and resurrection. We now look carefully at Rom 5:12-21, seeking to understand what God has done for us in the new creation.

Like all Jews, Paul accepted that 'in the beginning' (Gen 1:1) everything was exactly as God wanted it. God's glory and God's will were evident in creation and in the lives of Adam and Eve. But sin entered the world through Adam's disobedience. Once sin had begun, it gradually spread and took possession of the whole of God's originally perfect creation: 'Sin came into the world through one man' (v. 12). Long after the universal spread of sin, the Law was given to Moses. Sin abounded, and the Law could not free us from the slavery of sin (v. 13). It could protect us ... but not save us.

Paul, along with his Jewish contemporaries, believed that final salvation and the restoration of a world as God had made it would take place 'at the end' of all time. God would restore everything to its original beauty. Jewish belief was based upon the conviction that the loss of God's glory in the world because of the sin of Adam, at the beginning of all time, would be matched by the restoration of God's glory, at the end of all time. What was at the beginning – the glory of God – would be restored by God at the end.

But, as we have seen, Paul had been swept up into the power of Jesus' death and resurrection. These events took place during the course of ordinary human history – before the final end of time. Now Paul became a passionate believer that we did not have to wait till the end of time for God's way in the world to be re-established. God broke into the passage of ordinary human time in and through Jesus Christ. Jesus, taking on the sinful condition of human kind (Phil 2:7-8), reversed Adam's sin of disobedience by means of his unconditional obedience to God. Because of Jesus' death and resurrection, therefore, what had been expected to happen only at the end of all time was already happening:

Therefore, just as one man's trespass led to condemnation for all, so one man's act of righteousness leads to justification and life for all. For as by the one man's disobedience the many were made sinners, so by the one man's obedience the many will be made righteous (Rom 5:18-19).

This adversarial relationship between the disobedience of Adam, and its consequences of sin and death, and the obedience of Jesus Christ, with its consequences of an abundance of God's free gifts, leading to right relationship with him, explains what Paul means when he describes Adam as 'a type of the one who was to come' (v. 14). It is not that Jesus repeats Adam. He is only a 'type' in so far as he is an 'anti-type'. But what both Adam and Jesus Christ share is the *universal* effect of their contrasting responses to God. Adam's disobedience generated *universal* sin and death. Jesus Christ's obedience generated the possibility of *universal* right relationship with God.

Union with God and the fullness of life are now available. What Jesus had done for us introduced a 'new creation'. The beauty of God's original creation had been disfigured by sin. It has been restored in the new creation made possible by obedience unto death and the resurrection of Jesus. What was wrecked by one man's disobedience has been restored by another man's obedience.

This message is stated over and over (vv. 15-21), but Paul was an optimistic realist. The sinful condition established by the sin of Adam has not disappeared. The ruination of the original creation that set loose sin and death in the whole world is still abroad. It runs side by side with the grace and freedom established in the new creation made possible in Jesus Christ. We are called to choose which story we would like to join: that of Adam, or that of Jesus Christ.

CONCLUSION

Why do we still read the New Testament letters? I trust that this brief reflection upon the irreplaceable role of Paul, his authentic letters, and the letters that came into existence because of Paul's inspiration and the desire of a later generation to preserve his teaching, goes part of the way to answering that question. The choice before us, both individually and collectively, is 'Which story are you going to let be told in your life, in your world? Are you choosing death with Adam or life with Christ?' Not only selfish exploitation but even the attitude of 'going it alone' apart from God, no matter how well-intentioned, ranges one inevitably on the side of Adam. Surrender to God's gift of righteousness through faith in what God has done in and through Jesus Christ leads to life (Rom 3:21-26), becoming one with Christ (Phil 1:23-24), putting on Christ (Gal 3:27-28), in imitation of Christ (1 Cor 11:1), an instrument of fruit-bearing life (*cf* Col 1:3-6). It is only through reading the New Testament letters that we are made aware of this fundamental Christian truth.

CHAPTER SIX

The Gospels and the Eucharist

DONALD SENIOR CP

It is a joy to be able to honour Wilfrid Harrington, celebrating his exemplary life of scholarship at the service of the Church.

THE 'THEOLOGY OF THE LECTIONARY'

AS CLEARLY STATED in the official introduction to the Lectionary, the liturgical reforms of the Second Vatican Council wanted to reaffirm and intensify the place of the Gospels in the celebration of the Liturgy of the Word and within the entire Eucharistic celebration. First and foremost, in the liturgies for Sundays and Feast days the Gospel is the starting point for the selection of the reading from the Old Testament, intending to set up a thematic 'harmony' between the two. As the Introduction to the Lectionary states: 'The best instance of harmony between the Old and New Testament readings occurs when it is one that Scripture itself suggests. This is the case when the doctrine and events recounted in the texts of the New Testament bear a more or less explicit relationship to the doctrine and events of the Old Testament. The present Order of Readings selects Old Testament texts mainly because of their correlation with New Testament texts read in the same Mass, and particularly with the Gospel text' (n. 67).

This reflects the theological principle that the mystery of Christ revealed in the New Testament is mysteriously anticipated in the Old Testament and that the revelation found in the Old Testament Scriptures comes to its full expression in the New Testament, and in a particular way in the Gospels themselves. 'When in celebrating the Liturgy the Church proclaims both the Old and New Testament, it is proclaiming one and the same mystery of Christ. The New Testament lies hidden in the Old: the Old Testament comes fully to light in the New. Christ himself is the centre and fullness of the whole of Scripture, just as he is of all liturgical celebration. Thus the Scriptures are the living waters from which all who seek life and salvation must drink. The more profound our understanding of the celebration of the Liturgy, the higher our appreciation of the importance of God's word. Whatever we say of the one, we can in turn say of the other, because each recalls the mystery of Christ and each in its own way causes the mystery to be carried forward' (Introduction to the Lectionary, n. 5). This view is compatible, it should be noted, with a proper appreciation of the Old Testament as the revealed word of God in its own right – and not simply as an anticipation of the New Testament.

The instruction insists that the entire purpose of the Liturgy of the Word and its essential connection to the Liturgy of the Eucharistic sacrifice is to reveal the mystery of Christ and invite the faithful to participate in it through participation in the Eucharist. This reflection on the life of Christ takes place through the sequence of the liturgical year, which is primarily formed around the events of Christ's life but also in a unique way in the Gospel narratives themselves that appear in every Eucharistic liturgy. The liturgical year roughly tracks the sequence of events in Jesus' life: the anticipation of his coming during Advent, as the liturgical year begins; the events surrounding his birth during the Christmas season, the unfolding of his public ministry during Ordinary Time; the climactic events of the Passion and Resurrection during Lent, Holy Week and Easter; and the birth of the Church as the Easter cycle moves into the celebration of the feast of the Ascension and Pentecost, and in the selections from the early chapters of the Acts of the Apostles that mark the conclusion of the Easter cycle.

One of the most innovative liturgical reforms of the Council was to introduce a three-year cycle of selections from the Synoptics for the Sunday readings, with passages from the Gospel of John read every year. There is also a two-year cycle of sequential Gospel readings for the weekday Eucharists. Never before have Catholic congregations been exposed through the Lectionary selections to such a broad spectrum of the New as well as the Old Testament.

The instruction notes that the pride of place of the Gospel reading is reflected as well in the set of rituals that underscore its special importance. The Gospel book itself should be a work of artistic beauty (for a parish that can afford it!), worthy of being brought to a proper ambo in procession, honoured with incense and surrounding candles. The reading of the Gospel is to be introduced with music through the Alleluia verse and the conclusion of the Gospel reading also intoned to draw out the congregation's response. Only the ordained priest or deacon is authorized to read the Gospel passage.

The Word proclaimed is also to be the subject of the Eucharistic homily. More often than not in Catholic settings preaching focuses on the Gospel selection rather than on the Old Testament reading or on the selection from Paul or one of the other New Testament writings. It might be better if homilists ventured into these other parts of the Scriptures now and then, but at least if the homilist does given proper attention to the Gospel reading it reinforces the Church's concentration on the role of the Gospel readings in the Liturgy of the Word.

THE ORIGIN OF THE GOSPELS WITHIN THE LIFE OF THE EARLY CHURCH

This deep symbiosis between the Eucharist and the Gospel narratives fits well into the dominant Catholic perspective on the formation of the Gospels within the apostolic community and their nature as inspired and revealed texts. Official Catholic teaching has recognized a three-stage formative process that led to the emergence of the written Gospels (see, for example, the Pontifical Biblical Commission's 1964 document, Instruction on the Historical Truth of the Gospels; also the Second Vatican Council's *Decree on Divine Revelation*', n.19).

The first stage asserts that the ultimate origin of the Gospel tradition is rooted in the life of Jesus and his immediate disciples in the historical context of first century Palestinian Judaism. Key sayings of Jesus, his ministry of healing and exorcism, the basic contours of his life beginning in Galilee and concluding in Jerusalem, the essential Jewish character of so much of his life and teaching, the basic situation prevailing in the political, social and religious circumstances of Galilee and Judea, the events of his arrest and crucifixion in Jerusalem, and the witness of his resurrection – all of this basic data made an impact on the collective memory and consciousness of the earliest apostolic community and is detectable in the Gospels themselves.

The second stage is the transmission of this historical and theological memory of the first generation of 'eyewitnesses' and preachers of the word in the life of the early church. As Luke notes to 'Theophilus' in the preface to his Gospel, the 'events that have been fulfilled among us' were first 'handed on to us by those who from the beginning were eyewitnesses and servants of the word' (Luke 1:2). In preaching, catechesis, internal and external debate, and particularly – as we shall note further on – in the celebration of the Eucharist, the early community not only retained key traditions about Jesus and his ministry but, in the light of resurrection faith and the prophetic charisms of the authentic teachers of the early community, gave a profound theological and pastoral interpretation to this accounting of the life of Jesus. The Gospel stories and the sayings of Jesus were not simply archival material but an integral part of the church's proclamation, existing alongside other forms of Christian discourse such as the letters of Paul and the other New Testament writings being formed contemporary with this transmission of the Gospel material. It is likely that most of this Gospel tradition, as we might call it, was transmitted in oral form although certain parts of this tradition may have been put into written form prior to the third and final stage of the Gospel formation.

The third stage is the literary composition of the Gospels in essentially the same form as we have them today. Several converging factors may have triggered this new phase: i.e., the cataclysmic destruction of the Temple in 70 CE imposed a profound period of transition for both Judaism and Jewish Christianity; likewise there was the advancing time frame of Christian community itself when the first generations of Christian leaders were fading from the scene (this may be implied in Luke's own reason for deciding to write 'an orderly account'; see Luke 1:1-2) These and other factors led to the period when the Gospel tradition that up to this point was diffused and multiple in form and carried in a variety of settings would now be in a sense 'codified' in written form. Over time and yet fairly quickly, the early Church settled on the four canonical Gospels that are now part of the New Testament. The full canonical process and the official list of New Testament writings recognised by the church as authoritative and indeed 'inspired' would take a longer time to mature, but the essential roster of the four Gospels was rapidly set.

The precise interrelationship of the four Gospels continues to be sharply debated. Without trying to recapitulate the complexities of the so-called Synoptic problem here, we can offer the following sketch of what is a strong consensus that the Gospel of Mark was the first to be composed and to enjoy a certain apostolic status in the early community. In creating new versions of the Gospel, Matthew and Luke, independently of each other, absorbed much of the Gospel of Mark but also drew – again independently of each other – on a second source that appears to have been a collection of some sayings and parables of Jesus circulating in the early community – a collection rooted apparently in the Jewish Christian community, perhaps in the Galilean region and in the corridor of early Jewish Christian presence that extended north through Syria.

The consensus is more fragile concerning the relationship of John's Gospel to the three Synoptics. A classic view that still has support is that John indeed was acquainted with the Synoptic Gospels yet brings his own unique style and theological perspective to create a radically different form of the Gospel story (some evidence of possible contact pointed to are the similarities between John's passion narrative and the Synoptic version or the sequence of the multiplication of the loaves and the walking on the water which is similar to the same stories in the Synoptics). Others, however, affirm that John's Gospel represents a Gospel tradition independent of that which informed the Synoptic Gospels or that there was some interaction between these two streams of tradition prior to the literary composition of the Gospel narratives.

In any case, the emergence of the four Gospels from the living tradition of the early community is strong affirmed. The Gospels are, in a very true sense, the 'Church's book'. From a doctrinal point of view the conviction that the Gospel writings are 'inspired' needs to take into account not only the activity of the Gospel writers themselves but of the earliest communities who transmitted the Gospel materials which the evangelists later form into a coherent narrative whole.

THE EUCHARISTIC SETTING OF THE GOSPELS

The process of the formation of the Gospels briefly described above points as well to a profound connection between the Eucharist and the Gospels, giving a strong rationale for the pride of place given to the role of the Gospel readings within the Liturgy of the Word. In a very real sense, the Gospels were formed in the setting of the Eucharist and there find their most natural pastoral and theological context.

Recently, the Cistercian biblical scholar Denis Farkasfalvy has emphasized the Eucharistic origin of the Gospels.[1] He notes first of all that it is very likely that Paul's letters and other New Testament writings such as 1 Peter, Hebrews, Colossians, and Ephesians were first introduced to their audiences within the Christian assembly. The bearer of the letter would also elaborate on or offer commentary on the text that was being proclaimed to the assembly. The most natural setting for this would be the community's gathering for worship, particularly for the Lord's Supper or Eucharist. Evidence for this in the Pauline letters includes the many 'liturgical formulas' found in these texts: i.e., blessings (2 Corinthians 1:3-5), greetings (Romans 1:7), snatches of prayers and hymns (Philippians 2:5-11) which seem to presume that the letters would be read to the addressees in a liturgical setting. Farkasfalvy also appeals to Chapter 20 of the Acts of the Apostles which describes what might be a typical assembly of the early church who meet to 'break bread': a long presentation by Paul (enough to cause the young man

---

1. *Inspiration & Interpretation: A Theological Introduction to Sacred Scripture,* Washington DC, Catholic University of America Press, 2010.

Eutychus who was sitting in a window to fall asleep and tumble three stories to the floor below – only to be healed by Paul! See Acts 20:7-12) is followed by Paul's 'breaking bread and eating it' with the assembled Christians.

The connection between the Gospels and the early Eucharistic assemblies is more complex but no less compelling. It is likely that among the earliest part of the Gospel tradition to be formulated were the passion narratives, perhaps even taking shape within the Jerusalem church itself as it re-enacted the events of Jesus' final hours in a setting of prayer and reflection. Farkasfalvy notes that in each of the Synoptic passion narratives the gathering for the last supper and the so-called 'institution' account, with its strong Eucharistic overtones, serves as the major orientation or overture to the passion accounts. In the case of the Synoptic Gospels the last meal of Jesus with his disciples takes place within the passion narrative proper; for John, the 'institution' account is found in a different form in chapter 6 where the link between the 'bread of life' and the death of Jesus is also affirmed (see Jn 6:51) and at the last supper in chapter 13, the introduction to the Johannine passion narrative, there is the corresponding account of the foot washing (13:3-11). This link is echoed in Paul's own discussion of the Eucharist in 1 Corinthians 11 where in the course of his sharp reprimand for the abuses taking place at the Lord's Supper in that community Paul begins by recalling the memory of the passion story ('For I received from the Lord what I also handed on to you, that the Lord Jesus on night when he was betrayed took a loaf of bread …': 1 Cor 11:23-24).

Other features of the Gospels point to their Eucharistic provenance. The story of the multiplication of loaves appears in all four Gospels, with doublets of the story in Mark and Matthew, giving this incident a prominent role in the accounts of Jesus' mission. Jesus the Messiah, evoking memories of God's gift of the manna to feed the people in their desert trek, and the prophetic ministries of Elijah and Elisha who also miraculously fed people in need, feeds great multitudes with a few loaves and fish, acting out of compassion for 'sheep without a shepherd'. It is clear that the evangelist – or more properly the earlier tradition that had already shaped theses stories – makes a clear connection between the miracle of the feeding of the multitudes and the Eucharistic celebration. Jesus' gestures of 'blessing' the loaves, 'looking up to heaven', and 'giving thanks' (*eucharistein*) coincide with the Last Supper account and express an obvious liturgical tone, projecting the reader forward into the life of the Christian community itself as it gathers in the Eucharistic assembly.[2]

There is one other, more pervasive, characteristic of the Gospel materials that Farkasfalvy believes points to the Eucharistic setting in which these materials were first preserved and proclaimed. The Gospel accounts have a decidedly 'episodic' character. Jesus' public ministry is presented through a series of brief episodes – punctuated at times as in Matthew's Gospel by longer discourses – in which Jesus heals or encounters his opponents or interacts with his disciples. Jesus himself is on the move, an itinerant who goes from village to village, travelling on foot or by sea. He has, as Jesus notes in the Gospel of Luke, 'no place to lay his head' (Lk 9:58) In Mark's account, Jesus tells his disciples that he must be on the move to other villages to which he is sent (Mk 1:38). Much of the coherent narrative framework for the Gospel accounts as a whole is supplied in the introductions and conclusions to these brief episodes, often in generic phrases such as 'on the next day' or 'as they were going along the road' or indications that Jesus 'entered' a town or village and 'left there…'. Macro settings such as Judea, or the wilderness, or Galilee, or Jerusalem, or the 'Decapolis' further frame the account and give it its overall coherence and movement.

For the early form critics such as Karl Ludwig Schmidt, the main contribution of the evangelists was precisely to knit together these briefer episodes into an overall account, something like stringing beads on a string.[3] The later methods of redaction criticism and its refinement in what is called 'composition criticism' gave a more creative role to the work of the evangelist. While they did assemble brief narratives and some already formed blocks of material (e.g., the passion narratives), the evangelists also placed their imprint

---

2. On this link in the Gospel of Mark, see D. Senior, "The Eucharist in Mark: Mission, Reconciliation, Hope" *Biblical Theology Bulletin* 12 (1982) 67-72.

3. See his 1919 work, *Der Rahmen der Geschichte Jesu*.

on the content of the individual scenes, editing the stories in such a way as to contribute to their overall interpretation of the ministry of Jesus. In a parade example of this, Matthew's account of Jesus' walking on the water (14:22-33) differs significantly from the same story in Mark (6:45-52). Mark starkly emphasizes the failure of the disciples to understand Jesus' theophany on the sea while in Matthew, who characteristically softens Mark's portrayal of the disciples, the story ends with their acclamation of Jesus as Son of God (compare Mt 14:33 and Mk 6:51-52). The individual evangelists also made significant changes in the overall sequence of their narratives as a whole; for example, in the cases of Matthew and Luke, adding the infancy narratives and their strong connection to Israel and posing very different endings for their accounts (e.g., Luke ending with resurrection appearances in Jerusalem and the Ascension of Jesus; Matthew, with an appearance in Galilee and the dramatic commissioning scene at the very end of the Gospel).

The episodic nature of the Gospel materials points again to the likelihood that these materials were first presented within the context of early Christian liturgical assemblies. Along with the Pauline letters and other NT writings, the proclamation (or even enactment) of stories from the life of Jesus became the focus and reflection point for instruction and inspiration as the community gathered to 'break bread' with one another, to strengthen the bonds of the community, and to deepen their life of faith. As Farkasfalvy rightly notes, the protagonist in virtually every Gospel incident is Jesus. As the early Christians would encounter these stories in their assemblies they would instinctively identify with the original disciples and with the crowds who had come to Jesus for healing and inspiration.

In such presentations of a large selection of episodic material, Jesus is necessarily featured not merely as a figure of an objective past, defined and isolated in a frozen and distant temporal framework, but as the one who, at the beginning of an episode 'arrives' and becomes approachable once again, as the one who encounters the human needs and religious problems of living individuals, and, in these so-called 'limit situations' brings again the experience of salvation, that is, a manifestation of divine mercy, a solution unavailable from merely human resources.[4]

In this context of the early church's Eucharistic assemblies, the fund of traditions about Jesus and his mission rooted in the historical context of his original setting, now take on a powerful evangelical format, and ultimately would lead to the nature of the overall Gospel accounts fashioned by the evangelists. The effective and inspiring character of those full narratives would find a welcome reception within the community who could recognize the portrait of Jesus that they had come to know cumulatively in the course of their Christian worship. This aspect of 'reception' on the part of the community is often overlooked in some current discussions of the canonical process. As decisive for the canonical status of the four Gospels some scholars emphasize the role of imperial authority seeking uniformity, or the agendas of early Christian religious leaders such as Irenaeus wishing to impose doctrinal orthodoxy on the community and to bolster their own ecclesiastical authority. Whatever role such interests may have played in the process was entirely secondary to the more decisive role that the origin of the Gospel materials played within the context of Christian worship and the positive reception given to these particular portraits of Jesus by the Christian communities themselves and their rapid and widespread dissemination throughout the Mediterranean world. As Luke notes there seem to have been other attempts to provide narratives about Jesus' and his ministry (Luke 1:1) but it was these four that ultimately were received and retained by the early community and handed on with care to subsequent generations.

This scenario also has implications for another debate that has picked up steam in the ranks of biblical scholarship. Were the Gospels written for and directed to a local Christian community? Or, in the thesis of Richard Bauckham, were they originally written 'for the whole church'?[5] In other words, when Matthew composed

---

4. Farkasfalvy, 73.
5. *The Gospels for All Christians: Rethinking the Gospel Audiences* Grand Rapids: Eerdmans, 1998.

his Gospel was he writing it solely for the Christian community of Antioch (one of the prime candidates for the original setting of Matthew's Gospel) or from the outset did he intend his story of Jesus to have universal significance for the entire church? Placing the origins of the Gospels within the setting of early Christian Eucharistic celebrations, may enable the solution to this issue to be a 'both ... and'. The Gospel material originated in local communities and it is probable that the first appearance of the full Gospel narratives also took place in the setting of a local church's assembly. But given the track record of the circulation of key New Testament texts such as the Pauline letters or 1 Peter, and the widespread dissemination of stories about Jesus, it is likely that the authors of the Gospels knew that their accounts would be shared with other churches, even though they were first shaped for the circumstances of a local community. As suggested by the incorporation of the Gospel of Mark within the accounts of Matthew and Luke, as well as the shared use of the so-called Q document by both Matthew and Luke, and the probable contact at some point between the emerging Johannine tradition and the emerging synoptic tradition, there was from the outset a robust flow of materials and texts among the various early Christian communities.

PASTORAL IMPLICATIONS

This sketch of the origin of the Gospels within the Eucharistic assemblies of the early Church has some implications for the role of the Gospel readings within our Eucharist today. While reflection on the mystery of Christ is also present in the prayers, readings, hymns, and the Eucharistic prayer itself, surely it is the Gospel reading that is the most decisive element in reminding the congregation that the fundamental purpose of the Eucharist is to encounter again the presence of the Risen Christ in the midst of the Church and to remind us of our Christian identity as the Body of Christ. This should set the tone for all else that takes place in the Eucharist celebration, guiding the choice and quality of music, the appropriateness of the setting and ritual actions, and, above all, compelling the celebrant and homilist to keep the focus on Christ and nowhere else.

The nature of the Gospels as narrative and their central role in the Liturgy of the Word also reminds us of the power of story to move and inspire us – thereby reminding us that although the celebration of the Eucharist can also inform us and teach us, its primary purpose is to deepen our passion for God, to move us to a more profound and vibrant relationship with the Jesus who comes to us in the Eucharist, whose very being is entwined with us in communion, and whose grace can sustain us.

Finally, recalling that the Gospel materials, while drawing on traditions rooted in history yet were shaped in a Eucharistic setting, reveals to us the true nature of the Gospels as proclamation in narrative and thus should guide biblical scholarship within the community of faith. While the Church has repeatedly endorsed the historical critical method and affirmed the validity of using the various methods of historical, literary, and social-scientific inquiry to further understand biblical texts, the likely fact of the origin of the Gospel materials in a setting of worship reminds us that such methodology should be complemented by theological inquiry and by awareness of the sacred character of the biblical Word. The Gospels – and the Bible as a whole – remain the 'Church's book' and ultimately only in that setting can the full message of the biblical text come to light – a truth embodied in the scholar whom this volume honours.

CHAPTER SEVEN

God's Priestly Gospel: Preaching as Sacrifice
(*cf* Rom 15:16)

JEROME MURPHY-O'CONNOR OP

IN ASSIGNING ME the topic 'Preaching', the editor said 'we want to link the chapters in such a way that they will form a scriptural commentary on the Eucharistic liturgy, essays on biblical topics linked with the different parts of the Mass'. Immediately one Pauline text sprang to mind, because it fits this guideline perfectly. In Rom 15:16 Paul presents his preaching ministry as an act of cult by describing it in liturgical language. This text, however, presents certain challenges; the depth of its meaning does not appear at first sight. Thus I have chosen to reflect upon it as my tribute to Wilfrid, whose first class as a professor and mine as a student of sacred Scripture coincided in 1957. His enthusiasm and range of knowledge were key factors in my choice of career.

This journey into the past recalls another. In 2010 I celebrated my Golden Jubilee as a priest, and discovered that I had used 'God's gospel for my priestly charge', a paraphrase of Rom 15:16, on my ordination card. It summarizes the two aspects of the vocation that Wilfrid and I have lived out as priests in the Order of Preachers.

The NRSV translates Rom 15:15-16 thus:

[15]On some points I have written to you very boldly by way of reminder, because of the grace given me by God [16]to be a minister (*leitourgon*) of Christ Jesus to the Gentiles in the priestly service (*hierourgounta*) of the gospel of God, so that the offering of the Gentiles (*hê prosphora tôn ethnôn*) may be acceptable, sanctified by the Holy Spirit.

The renderings followed by a Greek word or words in brackets are the problem points, because in each case more than one translation is possible. Does *leitourgos* mean 'servant' in the ordinary sense or 'minister' with a cultic connotation? The genitive in Greek can bear many meanings. Thus does *hê prosphora tôn ethnôn* mean 'the offering which is the Gentiles' (genitive of apposition) or 'the offering made by the Gentiles' (subjective genitive)? On the surface, *hierourgounta* appears much less ambiguous, but the deeper one penetrates the more elusive the precise meaning becomes.

Leitourgos comes from the words *leitos* 'public, relative to the people' and *ergon*, 'work'. Thus *leitourgia* literally means 'public work'. Originally it was applied to anything done for the good of the people. Subsequently it came to express the duties that the State imposed on citizens capable of carrying them out. It was a type of 'forced labour' for those of wealth and intelligence, so burdensome in fact that many tried to escape. The corresponding verb *leitourgein* meant simply 'to work' in every sphere – whether simple manual labour, the artistic labour of musicians and actors, the liturgical action of priests in the sanctuary (*e.g.* Neh 10:37 = LXX 2 Esd 20:37), or the administration of governors.

It is against this background that we must look at Paul's usage. Epaphroditus was sent by the church at Philippi to bring financial aid to Paul, who describes him as 'your messenger and servant (*apostolos kai leitourgos*) to my need' (Phil 2:25) and 'one who risked his life to complete your service (*leitourgia*) to me' (Phil 2:30). Paul's use here of the prized title of *apostolos* (*cf.* 1 Cor 15:9) in the most basic sense of 'one sent' underlines how commonplace is the use of *leitourgos* here. The same purely secular sense appears when Paul speaks of civic duty in Romans, 'For the same reason you also pay taxes, for the authorities are servants of God (*leitourgoi theou*), attending to this very thing' (13:6). It is not that they have been directly mandated by God; the preservation of public order is manifestly a good thing, and so must be God's will.

Paul can also give this word-group a specifically religious connotation. Realizing that his imprisonment at Ephesus could lead to even greater humiliation, he nonetheless proclaims his serenity, 'Even if I am to be poured out on the sacrifice and service of your faith (*tê thysia kai leitourgia tês pisteôs hymôn*) I am glad and rejoice with you all' (Phil 2:17). 'Sacrifice and service' are grouped together as a hendiadys by the single definite article; they qualify each other reciprocally. In other words, 'service' is a form of 'sacrifice' and 'sacrifice' a form of 'service'. Clearly, the genitive is a genitive of apposition. The 'faith' of the Philippians is their 'liturgical sacrifice'. By 'faith' is meant, not the act of belief, but what Paul will elsewhere call 'the work of faith' (1 Thess 1:3; 2 Thess 1:11), which might be paraphrased 'faith in action, faith at work'.

The lifestyle of authentic Christians is a 'living sacrifice (*thysia*), holy and pleasing to God' (Rom 12:1). This is a typically Pauline paradox. When taken literally, a 'living sacrifice' is a contradiction in terms, because a sacrifice was effected by means of the immolation of the victim. Sacrifice was slaughter. Paul does not exclude the idea of death, yet what he has in mind here in Romans is a highly specific form of death:

> We were buried with him by baptism into death, so that . . .
> we too might walk in newness of life (6:4).

What Paul is suggestively evoking here he states explicitly in the Second Letter to the Corinthians:

> Always carrying in the body in the body the dying (*nekrôsis*)
> of Jesus, so that the life of Jesus may be manifested in our
> bodies. For we who live are being given up to death on
> account of Jesus so that the life of Jesus may be manifested in
> our mortal flesh (4:10-11).

The meaning of *nekrôsis* is disputed. The RSV translates it by 'death', no doubt because of the parallel in Rom 4:19, which speaks of the 'dead womb' of Sarah. It is better, however, to render it by 'dying' because it is obviously question of a process. Paul often thought that his last hour had come (2 Cor 11:23), and his list of the sufferings he endured (2 Cor 11:24-28) shows clearly how frequently the danger was indeed mortal. Consciously to live in the shadow of death is a form of 'dying'. Jesus, for his part, not only foretold his death, but had accepted that his death would be the means whereby his mission would be accomplished. As one marked for death, his whole life was a 'dying'.

The parallel between Jesus and Paul is very close. It is this that permits Paul to say that his *comportment* (notice the emphasis on 'body' and 'flesh', the antithesis of mere words) displays the 'life of Jesus'. The play on different senses of 'life' becomes intelligible when it is recognized that in the ancient world 'life' and 'death' could be used in three different senses: (A) physical, (B) existential, and (C) eternal. Philo, for example, wrote:

> Betaking myself for instruction to a wise woman, whose name is Consideration, I was released from my difficulty, for she taught me that some persons who are living (A) are dead (B) and that some who are dead (A) still live (C). She pronounced that the wicked, even if they arrive at the latest period of old age (A), are only dead (B), inasmuch as they are deprived of the life of virtue (B); but that the good, even if they are separated from all union with the body (A), live for ever (C), inasmuch as they have received an immortal portion (*De Fuga*, 55).

The 'life of Jesus' can only be understood in the existential sense, that is to say, in the way he lived. Paul knew a lot about the historical Jesus, but incidental references in his letters suggest that he was especially attracted by two aspects. The first was Jesus' total dedication to his ministry. Thus Paul mentions his 'steadfastness' (2 Thess 3:5), his 'fidelity' (Gal 2:16; 3:22; Phil 3:9); his life was an 'enduring Yes' to God (2 Cor 1:19), and this gave him the reliability of 'truth' (2 Cor 11:10). We have all known people so totally dedicated to one cause that to all others they were cold and harsh. This was not the case with Jesus, because Paul emphasizes his 'tenderness' (Phil 1:8), his 'meekness and gentleness' (2 Cor 10:1), and above all his 'love' (2 Cor 5:14), which expressed itself in the giving of self (Gal 2:20). This is the essence of a lifestyle that is a living sacrifice.

We might appear to have wandered far from Rom 15:16, but what has been said is indispensable to a correct understanding of the ambiguous phrase 'the offering of the Gentiles'. The genitive, as I pointed out above, can be read either subjectively or epexegetically. In the first case, it is question of a gift offered by the

Gentiles. Later on in this chapter Paul will speak of the collection he has organized among his Gentile churches for the poor of Jerusalem (15:25-30). Thus the 'offering of the Gentiles' could be their financial aid to fellow-believers in need.

This hypothesis is not without merit. While *prosphora* can carry a religious connotation (*e.g.* Acts 21:26), it can also have an entirely secular meaning. Consequently, it is perfectly appropriate to use it in reference to the collection. Moreover, in Rom 15:18, only two verses later, Paul speaks of 'the obedience of the Gentiles', and here the genitive is certainly subjective, because previously Paul had described faith as obedience (Rom 1:5). The similarity of the two phrases involving Gentiles might suggest that Paul is thinking of them in the same way. A further verbal link is to be found in the word 'acceptable' (*euprosdektos*), which occurs only three times in the Pauline letters, and, of those, twice in oblique references to the collection (Rom 15:31; 2 Cor 8:12). Finally, Paul uses *leitourgos* in Rom 15:16 and the cognate verb *leitourgeô* appears apropos of the collection in Rom 15:27.

These arguments yield evidence which fits rather than evidence which proves. In other words, if one has, *a priori*, opted for a reference to the collection, they offer confirmation. They do not, however, lead inexorably to that conclusion. A counter-argument that immediately comes to mind is the commonsense question, 'How could the readers of Romans have known that 'the offering of the Gentiles' was a reference to the collection, when Paul does not mention it until later in the chapter (15:25-30)? This, however, is not as watertight as might initially appear. Rom 16:3-4 shows that Prisca and Aquila were among the community in Rome to which Paul wrote. Earlier they had been with him in Ephesus (1 Cor 16:19) when he laid down how the collection was to be conducted (1 Cor 16:1-4). Thus they were fully aware of the collection and the importance that Paul attached to it (2 Cor 8-9). There is no hint that they had a mandate to request the participation of the Romans. That in fact would have been going too far. He had not founded the church of Rome, and the collection was to be a gesture from *his* churches. It would be surprising, however, if Prisca and Aquila had not spoken admiringly of Paul's project to bring aid to Jerusalem. One cannot assume that Roman Christians were unaware of the expectation laid on other Gentile churches.

Against the rather weak arguments that can be marshalled in favour of the subjective interpretation of 'the offering of the Gentiles', we must now see what can be said in favour of the majority opinion that it is the Gentiles themselves who are offered. One has only to read through Rom 15 to recognize that from v. 15 Paul's attention is focused entirely on himself. He is the only actor; the first person singular appears in virtually every verse. This makes it rather improbable that he would divert his readers' attention to the activity of someone else. On the contrary, the assumption must be that Paul thought of believing Gentiles as his offering. Hence, the genitive of apposition, 'the offering which is the Gentiles'.

The strongest confirmation of the correctness of this interpretation is what we have seen above regarding Paul's understanding of a Christ-like lifestyle in cultic terms. A life lived in imitation of Christ (1 Cor 11:1) is a form of sacrifical offering (Rom 12:1). Paradoxically, one text in Philippians brings together this idea and a gift of money. 'I have received from Epaphroditus the gifts you sent, a pleasing smell, a sacrifice acceptable and pleasing to God (*osmên euôdias, thysian dektên euareston tô theô*)' (4:18).

As Paul became more and more involved with the growing numbers of his converts, he had progressively less time to earn his living (2 Thess 3:8). Thus he became increasingly reliant on financial aid. He could not take it from the community in which he was currently living because it would impose on him the limitations of a client. It was acceptable only from communities that were now on their own. Then it was a gift of the church and not of any particular individual. As far as we know, only Philippi recognized his need, presumably because women occupied prominent positions in the church. They helped him when he worked in Thessalonica (Phil 4:15-16), in Corinth (2 Cor 11:9), and now in Ephesus (Phil 4:18). Grammatically, 'a fragrant offering, an acceptable sacrifice' refers to the financial aid sent by the Philippians, but commonsense dictates that what Paul appreciated was the generosity of his converts. Their comportment was 'the living sacrifice' that he required in Rom 12:1. The money was only the symbol of their deep and selfless devotion.

In the OT 'a pleasing smell' characterized burnt sacrifices, both of animals (*e.g.* Ex 29:18) and of incense (Ex 30:1-10; *cf* Lk 1:9). Primitive minds imagined the smoke ascending to heaven to delight the nose of God! Demonstrating how deeply rooted in Paul's consciousness was his cultic vision, he describes himself in the same terms as he speaks of his converts:

> [God] through us spreads the fragrance (*osmê*) of the knowledge of him everywhere. For we are the aroma (*euôdia*) of Christ to God among those who are being saved and among those who are perishing, to one a stench (*osmê*) from death (B) to death (C), to the other a fragrance (*osmê*) from life (A) to life (B) (2 Cor 2:14-16).

Osmé can be taken either positively (John 12:3) or negatively (Tob 8:3) according to the context; hence the differing translations in v. 16. The thematic links between this text and 2 Cor 4:10-11 (see above) are obvious, notably Paul's behavioural identification with Christ, and the play on the different senses of 'life' and 'death' (using the same initials as in the text we quoted from Philo). Paul's ministry, in other words, is a sacrifice pleasing to God; the odour becomes a stench in the nostrils of those who refuse his message.

Thus, despite the apparent detours we return very neatly to the key word in Rom 15:16, namely, *hierourgounta*. It is the present participle of the verb *hierourgeô*, which has only one meaning in biblical Greek (in classical Greek it is rare and late), 'to perform holy service, to act as a priest with regard to something' (BAGD[1]). It is this which confers a cultic dimension on the other terms in Rom 15:16, whereas its own meaning is intrinsic and does not depend on the context.

The given definition is based on a range of instances but it is imperative to distinguish the possible nuances that are found in contemporary texts. The high priest Matthias could not offer sacrifice (*hierourgein*) on Yom Kippur because he had a wet dream

---

1. Bauer, Arndt, Gingrich and Danker, *Greek-English Lexicon of the New Testament and Other Early Christian Literature*, 2nd ed., Chicago, 1979.

(Josephus, *Antiquities*, 17.166). This is the strictest sense. The one who sacrifices is a priest. But there were other possibilities. The arrows that the Roman legions fired into the Temple in 70 CE indiscriminately killed 'priests and those who offered sacrifices (*tois th'hiereusi kai tois hierourgousin)*' (Josephus, *War*, 5:16). The repetition of the article clearly distinguishes two groups, the priests and the ordinary lay people who brought victims to be sacrificed, as did Mary and Joseph (Lk 2:24). On another level, texts speak of Abraham 'sacrificing his son (*ton hyion hierourgôn)*' (Philo, *De Migratione Abrahami*, 67), and of Jephthah vowing to sacrifice (*hierourgein*) the first person from his house that he met on his return from his victory over the Ammonites (Josephus, *Antiquities*, 5.263). Neither was a priest, but they were prepared to give up what they held most dear. This, of course, is the sense in which we would say 'She sacrificed a career for marriage'.

There is no problem with the literal translation of *hierourgounta to euangelion tou theou* as 'sacrificing the gospel of God'. But in which of the three senses discerned above? It cannot be taken literally because Paul was not a priest. In fact 'priest' (*hierus*) is never predicated of any member of the early Church. Thus paraphrastic renderings which give prominence to a sacerdotal dimension should be excluded, *e.g.* 'in the priestly service of the gospel of god' (RSV, NRSV), 'the priestly duty of preaching the gospel of God' (NAB), 'serving the gospel of God as a priest' (Dunn), 'being the sacrificing priest of the gospel of God' (Sanday & Headlam).

Unfortunately neither of the other two senses seems appropriate. It is difficult to conceive of the gospel as a sacrificial victim like the Gentiles in the latter part of this verse. Nor is the preaching of the gospel something desirable to be surrendered in favour of a greater good, even union with Christ (Phil 1:23-24). The meaning intended by Paul is elusive, to say the least, and is perhaps best expressed in the ambiguity of the paraphrase 'ministering-in-sacrifice the gospel of God' (Richardson).

It is always difficult to pin down associative thinking, which is intended to be suggestive rather than precise. Two texts, however, provide useful clues as to what was going on in Paul's mind. The first is Rom 1:9, 'God is my witness whom I worship (*latrueô*) with my spirit in the gospel of his Son'. Paul claims that preaching the gospel is spiritual worship. For a person of his background the highest form of worship was sacrifice. Therefore, it was natural for him to think of his gospel in terms of sacrifice, without worrying about the precise nuance. The second is Paul's proud statement to the Corinthians, 'I begot you through the gospel (*dia tou euangeliou egô hymas egennêsa*)' (1 Cor 4:15). If this is put into the cultic context elaborated above, then the newness of life, which makes believers a new creation (2 Cor 5:17) and a 'living sacrifice' (Rom 12:1), comes into being through the instrumentality of the gospel preached by Paul. It is in this way that the Gentiles are 'offered as a sacrifice', and that idea is then attached to the gospel.

Why did Paul see his ministry, his life and the life of others in cultic terms? It must derive from his vision of the community as a spiritual temple. This concept is found in the Dead Sea Scrolls (1QS 8:5-9), but Paul did not borrow it from the Essenes. They arrived at the concept by different routes. Believing the temple in Jerusalem to be irredeemably corrupted the Essenes refused to participate in its rituals. They continued to pray, but felt the lack of sacrifice. Their solution was to consider prayer 'the offering of the lips ... a delectable oblation' (1QS 9:4-5; 10:6). Then it was a natural step to consider the place where such prayers were offered a spiritual temple. Paul would not have disagreed, but for him the temple was above all 'the house of God' (1 Kings 8:10-13), the place where God lived, and this is the aspect that Paul emphasizes: 'you are God's temple because God's spirit dwells in you' (1 Cor 3:16; 6:19). The fundamental activity of the temple, the response to God's presence, was sacrifice. Thus it was natural for Paul to think of all aspects of the life of the Christian community in sacrificial terms.

CHAPTER EIGHT

Creeds in Scripture and in Liturgy

LIAM G. WALSH OP

C HRISTIANS LIVE by faith. They live by faith in the Gospel of God that is embodied in Christ Jesus and given life in the believer by the Holy Spirit. The call to believe in the Gospel comes in words.[1] The reception in faith of the reality expressed in those words is a profound, all-encompassing commitment of self to God. And yet it too is expressed in words, as the proclamation was done in words. The act of reception is brought to consciousness and made deliberate in the saying of the words 'I believe', and the reality that is entered into by the decision to believe is put into the words that follow the 'I believe' and turn it into a sentence. While the subject of the sentence is the 'I' who believes, its object is the person being proclaimed in the Gospel: its object is 'God'.

The first sentence spoken by the believer runs, 'I believe in God ...' So the subject and object joined by the verb 'believe' are persons. What is being put into words is a personal relationship of the believer with God. Formulas of faith, then, such as the creeds are, are not first and foremost expressions of ideas. They are expressions of commitment to a personal relationship given between the believer and God. They are acts of the virtue that is called faith before being formulations of the doctrine of faith. They are made with particular force in the sacraments of faith celebrated in the liturgy. They will indeed be used as doctrine and sources of doctrinal development. Thomas Aquinas will say that the articles

1. Rom 10:6-18.

of faith that the creeds express provide the principles for all theology. But he will also say that the function of these formulae is to put the person who says them in touch with the reality of which they are the expression.[2] One does not believe in doctrines. One believes in God, Father, Son and Spirit. Believing, then, one achieves that personal oneness with God who is revealed as Father, Son and Spirit – a oneness that is called salvation. A reflection on the interaction of Scripture, liturgy and doctrine in the emergence and use of creeds in the community of believers should bear this out.

CONFESSIONS OF FAITH IN THE SCRIPTURES

Historically, the Christian practice of confessing faith in formulas of words had the important background of Judaism before it. Jewish people confess their faith in what has been called since Old Testament times the *shema Israel*. Observant Jews recite this prayer, within a setting of blessings, morning and evening. While the term *shema* is often used for the first six words of the formula, and this could well have been the original form of the *shema*, the full text is made up of three biblical texts: Deut 6:4-9; Deut 11:13-21; Num 15:37-41. It is a proclamation that the faith of Israel is centred on the only God, who is present in human life through his law, the *Torah*, in which salvation is to be found.

There is another classical confession of faith recorded in the Old Testament. Deuteronomy 26 describes the ritual presentation of first fruits that Israelites were required to make each year. When the priest had set down the basket of fruits before the altar, the one making the offering was to say: 'A wandering Aramean was my ancestor; he went down into Egypt … The Lord brought us out of Egypt with a mighty hand… and gave us this land, a land flowing with milk and honey. So now I bring the first fruit of the ground that you, O Lord, have given me' (Deut 26:5-10). This is a confession of faith in the God of Israel within an act of worship. The God being believed in is the Saviour of his people. His saving work is described in the story of his people, from Abraham to the present day. The telling of the story of Israel brings to light the real meaning

2. *Summa Theologiae* IIa-IIae, q.1, a.2 ad 2.

and reality of the basket of fruit being presented to God, turning this act of obedience to the Law into an experience of, and a laying hold of, God's saving work.

The *shema Israel* could have still served the first Christians to express their faith. They surely would have continued to proclaim its first six words: they believed in the one God of their Fathers. Their faith was faith in this God. They would have confessed their God as *Adonai*, the Lord. However, the term Lord was coming to have a specific meaning for them that it did not have in Jewish faith. Peter concluded his proclamation of the Christian Gospel on the day of Pentecost with the words, 'Let all the house of Israel therefore know assuredly that God has made him both Lord and Christ (NRSV: *Messiah*), this Jesus whom you crucified' (Acts 2:36). The confession of the one and only God as Lord is now occurring within the confession that this God, who is Lord, has made Jesus to be Lord. The distinctive faith in God of Christians is sometimes confessed in the Scriptures simply in the words 'Jesus is Lord.'[3]

LORD AND CHRIST

There is more to Christian faith that needs to be confessed. Peter's sermon in Acts 2 concludes that God has made Jesus both Lord *and Christ*. As the Christ he is the one in whom the divine work of salvation is definitively accomplished. The Jewish profession of faith in God was expanded from the original words of the *shema* to include biblical passages about the reality in which the saving work of God was accomplished for his people. Those biblical passages are about the Law. The Law was the way in which the covenant that God made with the Fathers of Israel, and that was codified through Moses, was given reality in the life of God's People. Jewish people believed in the Law as their way of divine salvation. The confession of Christian faith has to express the reality that a new covenant has been made in the blood of the crucified Jesus. He is the Christ, the anointed one, who brings the definitive gift of salvation. It is in the crucified one who was raised from the

---

3. See 1 Cor 12:3: ' ... no one can say 'Jesus is Lord' except by the Holy Spirit'; Rom 10:9: '... confess with your lips that Jesus is Lord'; Phil 2:11, 'every tongue confess that Jesus Christ is Lord'.

dead, and no longer in the Law, that salvation has now to be found. The story of the covenant, in which faith was confessed in Deuteronomy 26, has become the story of Jesus.

New Testament faith is in the story of Jesus, the Christ, in whom the new Israel comes into being. New Testament writings call Christians to believe in the salient happenings of the story of Jesus in which his being Lord and Christ are manifested. In a rather formal presentation of the Gospel in which Christians are called to believe, Paul marks the two key events in which the story begins and ends, right at the start of his Letter to the Romans: the Son 'was descended from David according to the flesh, and was declared to be son of God with power according to the spirit of holiness by resurrection from the dead, Jesus Christ our Lord' (Rom 1:3-4). The Gospel is about a real man, born of a human family, the family from which the Christ was expected to come; it is about someone who was raised from the dead and in so doing can be confessed to possess the holiness and power due to the Son of God. Speaking of this Christ Jesus later in the letter Paul says he is the one 'who died, yes, who was raised, who is at the right hand of God, who indeed intercedes for us' (Rom 8:34). Later, Timothy is told to remember Jesus according to these two Gospel events, although in reverse order: 'Remember Jesus Christ, raised from the dead, a descendant of David – that is my Gospel' (2 Tim 2:8).[4]

FATHER AND SON

The confession that Jesus is Lord and Christ was made by the first Christians within a faith in Yahweh, the God of Israel, the one and only God. When the Gospel was preached to the Gentiles it was still a call to belief in that one God, with a putting aside of the many gods of paganism. One finds biblical texts where the words about Jesus as Lord and Christ are combined with words about the one God confessed in a faith inherited from Judaism. Paul's introduction of himself and of his topic at the start of his letters regularly joins the proclamation of God and of Jesus (*e.g.* 1 Cor 1:1-3).

4. Other texts telling the story of Christ or details from it include, for instance, Gal 4:4, 1 Cor 15:3-5, 1 Tim 3:16, Phil 2:6-11.

Further on in First Corinthians Paul spells out more doctrinally this opening prayer addressed at once to God and to Jesus. In chapter 8, grounding his teaching about food offered to idols on the truth that there is only one real God, he proclaims 'for us there is one God, the Father, from whom are all things and for whom we exist, and one Lord, Jesus Christ, through whom are all things and through whom we exist (v.6)'.[5] Such formulations of Paul, and similar ones found frequently in the New Testament[6] are more than juxtapositions of words about God and about Jesus. The words used already give expression to belief in the relationship between the one confessed as God and the Jesus who is confessed as Lord. They already speak a truth that must always occupy the minds of believers. This truth will remain deeply mysterious even when its meaning is articulated more clearly in the formulas of faith that will be authorised in the post-apostolic Church. When these scriptural texts confess God to be Father they are using the personal name for God that Jesus favoured. He spoke of God as 'my Father'. The God that Jesus addresses as 'Father' is the One God of Israel. At the same time he is saying that there is something in the God of Israel and in himself, as Son of that Father, that makes them be one in a unique family bond that engages the very oneness of God. The Son is not the Father nor is the Father the Son and yet each is what the other is, because they are related as Father and Son. The Gospel of John gives the fullest and best articulated expression to this relationship between Father and Son, culminating in the words of Jesus 'I and the Father are one' (Jn 10:30).

The other relational feature between God and Jesus that is expressed in the text from the eighth chapter of First Corinthians is grounded on belief that God is the creator and purpose of all that is. The one God, the Father, is the one 'from whom are all things and for whom we exist' and Jesus is 'the one Lord ... through whom are all things and through whom we exist'. What the unique Father

5. *Cf* 1 Tim 2:5-7.

6. The texts given in this section on Scriptural confessions of faith are only a few of those that could be quoted (as they are, for example, in J.N.D. Kelly, *Early Christian Creeds*. London, Longmans, 3rd ed. 1972, chapter 1). The texts given here are chosen to illustrate the biblical phraseology out of which the Creeds will be predominantly formed.

does is done through the unique Lord. To confess this about Jesus is to affirm that he does not come forth from the Creator Father in the way all other things come forth. He is said in Colossians to be 'the first-born of all creation' in the sense that 'in him all things in heaven and on earth were created, things visible and invisible' (Col 1:15-17). He is said to be 'before all things' (Col 1:17). His coming forth is before the time of the created world began. In the Johannine writings his coming forth is described as that of the 'only begotten of the Father' (Jn 1:14), 'the only begotten Son' (Jn 1:18, 3:16, 18).

FATHER, SON AND SPIRIT

The faith of Christians in the God who is the Father of the Lord Jesus Christ is a faith that brings them salvation. It was for that salvation that the Father sent his Son, and that the Son lived, died and rose to the glory of God the Father. In the Scriptures of the New Testament, the manifestation of that salvation in the transformed lives of Christians is attributed again and again to the Spirit of God, to the Holy Spirit given to those who are saved. Paul writes, for example, that 'God's love has been poured into our hearts by the Holy Spirit that has been given to us' (Rom 5:5).[7] The making visible of the Spirit occurs in the experience of Christians, collective and individual. The identity of that Spirit is expressed in affirmations, including these: that it comes from God, is the Spirit of God, and that it comes from Christ Jesus and is given in and by him to those being made holy. While the term 'spirit' can sometimes seem to designate a transforming power that comes forth from God, it is spoken of frequently in ways that give it a personal status. The Spirit does things for, to, and in Christian believers. The believer relates to the Spirit personally. The One related to becomes part of the believer's confession of faith in God. There are texts in which belief in the Spirit is combined with belief in Christ the Lord and in his work of salvation, and with God, the Father of the Lord and Christ. Paul writes: 'There are varieties of talents, but the same Spirit, varieties of service, but the same Lord, and varieties of effects, but the same God who effects everything in everyone' (1 Cor 12:4-

---

7. See also Rom 14:17; 1 Cor 2:12; 1 Pet 6:14.

6), and 1 Peter addresses itself to those 'who have been chosen and destined by God the Father and sanctified by the Spirit to be obedient to Jesus Christ …' (1 Pet 1:2).

That the Christian confession of faith entails recognising God the Father, Jesus the Lord and Christ, and the Spirit the Sanctifier is expressed in two texts that make the three who are being confessed stand out quite clearly. In 2 Cor 13:14 Paul writes: 'The grace of our Lord Jesus Christ, and the love of God, and the communion of the Holy Spirit be with you all'. And in Mt 28:19 Jesus commands: 'Make disciples of all nations, baptising them in the name of the Father and of the Son and of the Holy Spirit'. Three are named, three in whom the reality of God is recognised, but with differences expressed in three names. There is no sense that God is being multiplied. The names used of the three are relational names: one cannot be conceived or spoken about without the others. Christian faith in God is expressed when each of the three is confessed.

CONFESSIONS OF FAITH AND THE LITURGY

Exegetes note that the biblical texts put forward here as confessions of faith often seem to include phrases that are invested with a certain ring of familiarity. Some even use the expression 'catch-phrase' to describe them. The Christian community must have had such familiar phrases that would come readily to the mind of someone such as Paul writing to that local Church about its life and practices. These phrases would have been the staples of the catechetical instruction in 'the doctrine of the Apostles' that would have been given to those coming to faith and preparing for baptism. In a more public way they could have become familiar by being used when the community gathered regularly for its celebrations of the memory of Christ. The celebration of baptism would have been such an occasion. When at the end of the Gospel according to Matthew, the command of Jesus to baptise those who were being made disciples is made specific as being a baptism 'in the name of the Father and of the Son and of the Holy Spirit' it is clear that the faith confessed in baptism by those for whom Matthew wrote was faith in God, named Father, Son and Spirit. Other scriptural texts tell what the three have done and how they relate to each other. In telling their story those texts have identified who and what Father, Son and Spirit are, have given them the personal identity that is assumed in calling them by name and being baptised in their name. The texts could well have been constructed from phrases made familiar in the course of the preaching that Jesus prescribed when he said 'make disciples of all nations'. They surely underpinned any formula in which faith was confessed at the moment when his command '… baptising them …' was fulfilled.

There is an addition in the Western recension of Acts to the story of the conversion of the Ethiopian eunuch by the deacon Philip (Acts 8:35-38) that might reflect a connection between New Testament formulations of faith and baptism. Philip has evangelised the eunuch by explaining to him the meaning of the Scriptures. The recognised text says '… they came to some water; and the eunuch said "Look here is water. What is to prevent me from being baptised?"' Here the Western recension adds a dialogue between Philip and the eunuch: 'And Philip said "if you believe with your heart you may". And he replied "I believe that Jesus Christ is the Son of God"'. Then Philip baptises him. Scholars think the Western addition to the text might well reflect a sequence of moments that had become established in a baptismal liturgy. Candidates ask to be baptized ('What is to prevent me from being baptized'). They are told that the only thing that could still be lacking (other obstacles could have been removed by a process that will eventually become the catechumenate) is faith in the Lord Jesus. Once they confess that faith they are baptised in it.

WRITINGS OF THE SECOND CENTURY

Patterns and phrases for confessing faith such as have been found in the New Testament are found again in the writings of the Apostolic Fathers. Suggestions that they came from established summaries of doctrine such as would eventually evolve into what are called 'declaratory creeds' do not appear to be convincing.[8] What

8. On this issue see Kelly, *Early Christian Creeds*, 30ff.

seems more likely is that the first standardised formulations of faith occurred, not as instruments of Church teaching but in the baptismal liturgies of the churches. The second century authors would have drawn their inspiration from these liturgies and filled them out with details from the tradition of preaching and teaching by which the Church lived. In drawing from the tradition they would have shaped the baptismal formulas of faith according to the need to deal with the catechetical or doctrinal issues that concerned them. Out of these developed formulations the creeds would have emerged. The credal forms of confession could, in turn, have found their way back into the liturgical usage.

Something of this sort can be seen in St Ignatius of Antioch whose concern to overcome Docetist thinking about Jesus is made clear in passages in which he lists details of the human existence of Jesus – his being born of the Virgin, eating and drinking, baptised by John, nailed to the cross under Pontius Pilate, raised from the dead. His texts reflect existing Christological confession of faith, but they also fill these out in ways that will find their way into creeds, as well as into baptismal liturgies.

In the information he gives about what Christians believe and practise, the apologist St Justin regularly presents the faith they profess according to the Father, Son, Spirit pattern that emerges in the New Testament; but occasionally, also in conformity with New Testament usage, he presents it in purely Christological terms. Suggestions that Justin is drawing from a primitive formulation of the creed of the Church of Rome do not seem to be convincing. What seems more likely is that his source for these formulations is the Church's liturgy. Two of the 'trinitarian' confessions come in Justin's descriptions of the Eucharist, two more come from his account of how people are baptised.

Justin does not describe how the confession of faith is actually done in the liturgy of baptism. Later evidence, such as can be found in St Irenaeus, Tertullian and *The Apostolic Tradition* attributed to St Hippolytus, indicates that it was done in the form of responses by the one being baptised to a set of questions put by a minister of the Church concerning faith in Father, Son and Spirit. In responding affirmatively to the questions 'Do you believe in God the Father almighty ... Do you believe in Jesus Christ the Son of God who was born ... Do you believe in the Holy Spirit, in the holy Church and the resurrection of the flesh ...' the one to be baptised confessed the faith and was baptised.

DOCTRINE

The evidence that it is the liturgy that provides the structured confessions of faith from which second century Christian writers draw is often put forward within a thesis that creeds in the form that we know them now – often called 'declaratory' creeds – did not come into existence until the third and perhaps fourth century.[9] While the historical question of the origin of creeds that are somehow independent of liturgical usage is important, there is a theological issue that can be somewhat obscured by this historical discussion. The debate can carry the risk of turning the distinction between 'declaratory' creeds and baptismal confessions of faith into some kind of opposition, as if they belonged to two separable activities of the Christian Church – the one liturgical, the other doctrinal.

The undoubted priority that has to be given to baptismal usage in understanding the origin and development of the historical creeds in no way excludes the presence of doctrinal concerns from the beginning of the story, as is evidenced in the Scriptures and in the Fathers of the second and third centuries. There was a need to get it right, to tell the truth about Jesus, about the God who is his Father, about the Spirit who is present and given in the interaction of Father and Son.[10] This need was surely felt, and was at its most demanding, in the confession of the faith that the Church made when it baptised someone. The baptising Church had to be clear about the one in whose name it was baptising, and the one being baptised had to be clear about who and what are the Father, Son and Spirit with whom he/she was entering into relationship.

Baptism was, indeed, a ritual and obeyed the laws of ritual activity. The washing, anointings, laying on of hands, stripping and

9. *ibid.*
10. See Frances Young, *The Making of the Creeds*, London, SCM Press, 1991, especially Introduction and Chapter 1.

putting on of significant garments, kisses of peace, all operated symbolically. But their Christian symbolism depended on facts, not on mythical fictions. It depended on things that God really did, does, and will do, and on what God revealed about himself in doing so. To believe was to affirm the truth of these events and the truth about the one revealed to be at work in them. It was in that affirmation that the personal relationship that saving faith set up between God and the believer occurred. Affirming the truth about God, and consequently the untruth of the gods of the nations, was built into the faith of Israel. Affirming the truth about Jesus as Son of God became a requirement of this faith for Christians, and distinguished them from Jewish believers. As the Gospel came to be preached in the pagan Greco-Roman world, the need to affirm the truth about God became still more demanding. People being baptised had to be liberated from a mind-set that had them thinking in terms of *many* gods.

The source of the doctrinal content of the confessions of faith is the tradition of apostolic faith that is canonised in the Scriptures. As the canonical status of the Scriptures became recognised throughout the Church, the authority of the scriptural words and phrases became imperative. But concerns about meaning and coherence were at work in the way they were put together in the formulas of confession. The threefold pattern of Father, Son, Spirit provided by the Scriptures was an obvious principle of organisation, especially in view of the command of Jesus to baptise in the name of the Father, the Son and the Holy Spirit.

What had to be said about the Father also came from the Scriptures. But the choices made were influenced by doctrinal concerns. For example, the adjective 'omnipotent' begins to appear regularly. The uniqueness of the God of Israel was bound up in Jewish faith, at least from the time of the Exile, with belief that this is the God who creates the world and manages its historical destiny. The all-powerfulness of God, so often celebrated in the Bible, is affirmed in the Greek and Latin words that are translated 'omnipotent.' The words served Christians, mindful of their Jewish origins and then of the pagan world in which they were coming to live, to affirm the uniqueness of God in the one they called Father. Very soon the more specific term 'creator' will be introduced, and the range of God's creative action will be confessed by phrases like 'of heaven and earth', or 'of all things, visible and invisible.' The need to free Christian faith from the distortions of Gnostic speculation that separated the Father God from the Demiurge creator who made the despised material world was also met by identifying the Father of Christian faith as the omnipotent creator of all things, material as well as spiritual.

The concern of Ignatius of Antioch to correct Docetist thinking about the Son has already been noted. The need to affirm the true historical humanity of Jesus and the historical reality of the events of his life is given expression in the Christological development of the confessions about the Son. It is done in a series of historical statements, all drawn from the New Testament: he 'was born', he 'suffered, died and was buried', he 'was raised ... ascended ... sits ... will come to judge.' These are affirmations of fact, of events past, present, and to come attested by the Scriptures. The concern is with the truth of things and the reality of what is being affirmed.

Facts are harder to identify when it is the reality of the Spirit that is being confessed. St Justin said Christians are baptized in the name of the Spirit 'who through the prophets announced beforehand the things relating to Jesus'. It is by a presence in, an activity through the prophets, and a fulfilment of what they announced in Jesus, that he identifies the Spirit. Already in the second century other manifestations of the presence and action of the Spirit in relation to Jesus and his work are being added in confessions of faith in the Spirit. They are events of the human story in which the divine Spirit is present, manifested, and at work. They are realities in which the fruits of the divine work done in Jesus is realised in the lives of those he came to save. They are, once again, realities proclaimed in the Scriptures. They are the Church, the remission of sins, the resurrection of the body into everlasting life. They are realities in which the Spirit is manifestly present and at work. They give realism to the confession of faith in the Spirit and give the Spirit a personal identity.

CREEDS, LITURGY, AND DOCTRINE

What has been presented here is only the beginning of the story of what are properly called creeds. If the story were fully told it would be about the fixing of credal formulas, about their use in the *traditio symboli* and *redditio symboli* during the catechumenate, about the use of *symbolum* to speak of creeds and the various explanations of what that word meant. It would speak about the importance attached to the creed used by a church in verifying its place in the communion that the churches enjoyed when they gathered at synods and ecumenical councils; it would be a story about the choice of a particular baptismal creed and its doctrinal refinement to deal with the divisions caused by the Arian heresy at the Council of Nicea and the subsequent filling out and adoption of that creed to become the Creed of Nicea-Constantinople. A fuller presentation of this development would also deal with the doctrinal force of that Creed in maintaining the ecumenical communion of the churches, and with its entry into the liturgy of the Eucharist, first in the East and then in the West; it would tell about the persistence and acceptance by the churches, side by side with the Creed of Nicea-Constantinople, of the baptismal creed of the Roman Church that came to take the form known as the Apostles' Creed. The story would bear out the central role of the creeds in the way the teaching of the Scriptures has been summarised, maintained and had its meaning clarified in the tradition of Church life, a tradition that is interactively liturgical and doctrinal, that is at once *lex orandi* and *lex credendi*.

Part Three

CELEBRATING THE EUCHARIST

Elijah and the Raven

CHAPTER NINE

The Prayers of the Liturgy

THOMAS O'LOUGHLIN

'Now give thanks, blessing God thus ...'

WITHIN A FEW DECADES of the first Easter the basic form of Christian prayer had taken shape – and this form still underpins virtually all our prayer at the Eucharist. In the *Didachê*, which represents the earliest stratum of prayer practice at the Christian community meal[1], we find this prayer supplied as a model for the Christian householder to offer what is already being described as the sacrifice of praise:[2]

> Now this is how you should engage in giving thanks,
> bless God in this way. First, at the cup, say:
> We give thanks to you, our Father,
> for the holy vine of David, your servant,
> which you have made known to us.
> Through Jesus, your servant, to you be glory forever (IX:1-2).[3]

---

1. On the Eucharist as an event within the regular community meals of the earliest churches, see the work of P.F. Bradshaw, *Reconstructing Early Christian Worship*, London 2009, 3-53; and A.B. McGowan, 'Naming the Feast: Agape and the Diversity of Early Christian Meals,' *Studia Patristica* 30 (1997) 314-8. On the dating of the *Didachê*, see T. O'Loughlin, 'Reactions to the *Didachê* in early twentieth-century Britain: a dispute over the relationship of history and doctrine?' in F. Knight, et al., eds, *Festschrift* for Prof. Keith Robbins (forthcoming).

2. See A. Milavec, 'The Purifying Confession of Failings Required by the Didachê's Eucharistic Sacrifice,' *Biblical Theology Bulletin* 33 (2003) 64-76; and cf. J.P. Audet, 'Literary Forms and Contents of a Normal Eucharistia in the First Century', in K. Aland et al., eds, *Studia Evangelica*, Berlin 1959, vol. 1, 643-62

3. The translation is taken from T. O'Loughlin, *The Didachê: A window on the earliest Christians*, London 2010, and see 85-104 for further details on their Eucharistic practice.

And the pattern is immediately repeated:

Then when it comes to the broken loaf say:
We give thanks to you, our Father,
for the life and knowledge you have made known to us.
Through Jesus, your servant, to you be glory forever (IX:3).

The fact that it seems so familiar can lead us to underestimate the degree to which it shows a community already using a radically Christian prayer at its Sunday meal. Meanwhile, the similarities of these prayers with what we can determine about the forms of Jewish meal prayers can mask the extent that it represents a major shift in the theological self-understanding within the earliest communities.[4]

Blessing God in gratitude for food was hard-wired into the notion of the covenant. (It is of course God, not the food to hand, that is 'blessed'.) It was God who had given his people 'a land flowing with milk and honey' (Deut 26:15) and it was this gift of the land that was the basis of all other gifts, including the food it produced. For this, his goodness, God was to be praised. At a meal, then, while the food on the table was the occasion of the thanksgiving prayer, the thanksgiving was not confined to what was on the plates, but extended to *all* God's gifts, the whole creation.[5] The actual meal was a sacrament of all food, indeed of all of God's gifts to his people. It is with this meal practice that Jesus and the first followers would have been familiar.[6] However, when we look again at the *Didachê* we see that three important changes have taken place.

In the first place, God is addressed in a formal prayer as 'Father.' This, in itself, is not surprising as it is the basis of relationship that Jesus established between his community and God.[7] This is the

4. The fundamental work is L. Finkelstein, 'The Birkat Ha-mazon,' *Jewish Quarterly Review* n.s. 19 (1929) 211-62; and cf. E. Mazza, *The Origins of the Eucharistic Prayer* Collegeville, MN 1995, 16-26.

5. See B.M. Bokser, 'Ma'al and Blessings over Food: Rabbinic Transformation of Cultic Terminology and Alternative Modes of Piety,' *Journal of Biblical Literature* 100 (1981) 557-74.

6. See D.E. Smith and H.E. Taussig, *Many Tables: The Eucharist in the New Testament and the Liturgy Today,* London 1990; H.E. Taussig, *In the Beginning was the Meal: Social Experimentation and Early Christian Identity,* Minneapolis, MN 2009.

7. On the rapidity with which the appreciation of the Eucharistic meal as an encounter

sonship that formed them as a new people who could call out 'Abba! Father' (*cf* Rom 8:15), and it is as such a community that the *Didachê* 8:3 prescribes that they pray the 'Our Father' three times daily.

Secondly, instead of the prayer referring to the gift of the food there before them and, by extension, all God's gifts, now the thanksgiving ignores (verbally) the food and is solely concerned with the Father's gift of his Son. The food in the presider's hands is not even mentioned – yet the food is still the occasion of the prayer – and so has in effect become a sign of the Father's new gift. This sacramentality of the food is then confirmed in the *Didachê*'s next chapter where the nature of a loaf of bread becomes, itself, representative of the new covenant group[8] with Jesus: 'For as the broken loaf was once scattered over the mountains and then was gathered in and became one, so may your [the Father's] church be gathered together into your kingdom from the very ends of the earth' (9:4). This is the same identification between the loaf and the gathering that Paul invokes in 1 Cor 10:16-7: 'The loaf which we break, is it not a participation in the body of Christ? Because there is one loaf, we who are many are one body, for we all partake of the one loaf.'

Thirdly, these prayers in the *Didachê* are not simply offered to the Father by the group, but offered through Jesus – indeed, we see the familiar formula *per Christum Dominum nostrum* in the course of formation in its repeated use in the text. It is the prayer of Christ to the Father, and the community (transformed and bound together in him by baptism like the grains of wheat transformed and bound into a loaf) are enabled to be there, and pray thus, through him. Although the *Didachê* does not employ a priestly language about Jesus, and although it does see the Eucharist as the community's

---

with the risen Jesus developed, and thus that he could present the community to the Father, see T. O'Loughlin, 'Another post-resurrection meal, and its implications for the early understanding of the Eucharist', in Z. Rodgers, M. Daly-Denton, and A. Fitzpatrick-McKinley eds, *A Wandering Galilean: Essays in Honour of Seán Freyne* Brill, Leiden 2009, 485-503.

8. The use of the word 'bread' rather than 'loaf' is a legacy of the Scholastics, and distracts from the fundamental significance of the loaf; see T. O'Loughlin, 'Translating Panis in a Eucharistic Context: A Problem of Language and Theology,' *Worship* 78 (2004) 226-35.

sacrifice,[9] we can notice that their liturgy already contained elements that could form the basis of the priestly Christology used by the author of Hebrews: 'Through him then let us continually offer up a sacrifice of praise to God, that is, the fruit of lips that acknowledge his name' (13:15).

The structure of prayer in the *Didachê* can be summarised thus: at the community's meal, there takes place their act of Eucharist, the Father is blessed for the gift of the Christ, and this blessing by the Church is made in and through the Christ. This was to become, if it had not done so already, the paradigm for all liturgical prayer.

AN INCARNATIONAL PATTERN

This basic pattern of blessing and thanking God (the *euchological* pattern) found in the *Didachê* is not simply a matter of ritual style or of linguistic convention – normally significant factors in the generation of liturgical elements – but was seen to reflect the community's faith and their existential reality as the people of the new covenant. In sending them Jesus, his child, God had revealed himself as their Father. This child was not just another gift but was the gift beyond gifts: greater than Moses and Elijah (Mk 9:4), greater than David (Mt 12:3-4), than Solomon (Mt 12:42), the Temple, or even the Sabbath (Mt 12:6-8). This was the gift for which thanks was offered first and foremost: all other reasons for thankfulness could now be seen in relation to the gift of this child. Further, because Jesus was the one who established this new covenant community, the community did not act for itself, but in union with him. As disciples they sought to walk 'the way' of the Lord, and then through him they offered the eschatological sacrifice of praise.[10] In Jesus coming among them and constituting them as a people, they had glimpsed the pattern of God's creating and self-revealing action, and the structure of their prayer was a response that echoed the action. Later on that pattern was filled out with a more elaborate Christology, and its Trinitarian structure made more explicit with the addition of a reference to the Spirit. But the basic theological, as well as ritual, form of Christians' prayer had taken shape.

9. See Milavec, *loc. cit.*, for a perceptive study of this issue.
10. See Mal 1:11, echoed in Didachê XIV:3 (*cf* O'Loughlin, *The Didachê*, 129-30).

With just a few exceptions, this pattern repeats itself throughout the liturgy today. It can be most clearly seen in the Eucharistic Prayers. Each of these begins with an address to the Father using the formula:

Father, all-powerful and ever-living God,
we do well always and everywhere to give thanks,
through Jesus Christ our Lord.[11]

Then, of all the Father's gifts, it is the gift of the Son that is placed at the centre of the prayer by recounting the memory of his paschal mystery. The whole prayer concludes with the doxology when, through, with, and in the Son, the Church offers 'all glory and honour' to the Father. This pattern is not to be seen as a template, as if each and every Preface-and-Eucharistic Prayer were simply a verbal variation on the theme. Rather it is the structure that lies embedded within the many Prefaces and Prayers – and the number and variety of both has increased enormously within western Christianity since the reforms of the Second Vatican Council – and gives them their profound unity as 'Eucharistic Prayers.'

The pattern also manifests itself in the 'little prayers' that go to make up each celebration of the Eucharist. Here is a very clear example from the Dawn Mass for Christmas:

Father, we are filled with new light
by the coming of your Word among us.
May the light of faith shine in our words and actions.
Grant this through our Lord Jesus Christ, your Son,
who lives and reigns with you and the Holy Spirit,
one God, for ever and ever.

The Father is addressed, and then it is his greatest gift which forms the basis of our expression of desire for 'the light of faith,' and then the Son is mentioned in the concluding formula by which we declare that this is our prayer only in the sense that we are in union with the Christ. The first and third elements are absolutely

11. [*Editor's note, relating to this quotation from the Missal and the other further down this page:* This translation was in use until just before Advent 2011, but it suits the author's point here in a way that would not be so clear in the newer version.]

stable (whether it is in an Opening Prayer, a Prayer over the Gifts, or a Prayer after Communion), but the second element – that the praise is for the gift of the Son – varies over the course of the full year's liturgy particularly in the two latter prayers. Take, for instance, this Prayer over the Gifts:

> ... accept the offerings of your Church,
> for in your mercy you have given them to be offered...
> Through Christ our Lord.[12]

Here the actual gifts are the focus of attention rather than the Christ-event, but all such variations do not distract from the overall structure as none of these items is intended for use as stand-alone prayers: each belongs within the community's overall Eucharistic activity. All the prayers point out that it is the Father who is addressed, the 'destination' of our prayer, and we are enabled to do this because we are 'in Christ' – the community is, rather than a collection of individuals[13]

Perhaps the least appreciated prayer in the liturgy is the Prayer of the Faithful (*Oratio Fidelium*).[14] Because it can be omitted it tends to be seen as 'an optional extra' and so downgraded to being an incidental item that can take any form we choose.[15] However, we stand as the priestly people before the Father when we make this prayer, and so it is an ecclesial action of the first order as we make intercession for ourselves, for the world, and for the whole creation. Theologically, this prayer locates its basis in the reality of the whole community being the new priestly community through baptism – hence it is the prayer of the faithful – and the ritual is a recollection of the high priest entering the Holy of Holies.[16] But we are a priestly

---

12. *Roman Missal*: Nineteenth Sunday in Ordinary Time.

13. See O. Casel, *The Mystery of Christian Worship*, new edition by B. Neunheuser with introduction by A. Kavanagh, New York, NY 1999.

14. Note that it is not the *orationes fidelium* as if it were simply a collection of petitions, yet we commonly refer to it as 'the prayers of the faithful', or even less appropriately as 'the bidding prayers' which is but a material description of part of its content.

15. See T. O'Loughlin, 'Liturgical Evolution and the Fallacy of the Continuing Consequence,' *Worship* 83 (2009) 312-23.

16. See F.H. Gorman, Jr, *The Ideology of Ritual: Space, Time and Status in the Priestly Theology* Sheffield 1990.

people because of our union with the Great High Priest, and we utter this prayer in the liturgy within the framework of Jesus entering the perfect sanctuary spoken of in Hebrews 9. The next chapter of Hebrews specifies this is the sanctuary we too can 'enter with confidence through the blood of Jesus' (10:19). So standing together at the liturgy we stand in the presence of God and ask for whatever we need. But if we address the Father, we do so only because we have been formed into a priestly people through the coming of the Son and our union with him in baptism. Then, voicing our intercessions, 'exercising [our] priestly function by interceding for all mankind ... for the Church, for civil authorities, for those oppressed ... and the salvation of the world,'[17] we act 'through Christ our Lord.' So this prayer, too, can be seen in its own way to exhibit the fundamental euchological structure.

The few cases when prayer in the liturgy does not exhibit this structure are instances where the 'exceptions prove the rule'. There are, it is true, intercessions addressed to the Lord Jesus in the penitential rite of the Eucharist, but in the Liturgy of the Eucharist itself, the only regular feature where prayer is not addressed to the Father are the texts beginning 'Lord Jesus Christ you said to your apostles' after the Prayer taught by the Lord Jesus and the two similar prayers that form part of the president's private preparation before Communion. The oldest of these prayers date from the ninth century[18] when the notion of the Mass as the personal act of the priest on behalf of others had already replaced the notion of the whole Church's Eucharistic action.[19] In the pre-1970 rite all three occurred together and there have been minor changes, somewhat inappropriately, in the reformed rite because abandoning them seemed too big a shock to sacerdotal piety in the late 1960s. The changes took the form of making the first prayer plural: the *ne respicias peccata mea* [of the president] became *peccata nostra* [of the community), while, whichever of the second two is used, is to be

17. *General Instruction on the Roman Missal*, 45.

18. J.A. Jungmann, *Missarum Sollemnia: The Mass of the Roman Rite*, New York 1955, vol. 2, 345.

19. T. O'Loughlin, 'Treating the "Private Mass" as Normal: Some Unnoticed Evidence from Adomnán's De locis sanctis,' *Archiv für Liturgiewissenschaft* 51 (2009) 334-44.

said *secreto*. These are an evolutionary anomaly, a witness to the poverty of medieval appreciation of the Eucharist as an event, and so do not challenge the basic form.

The other exceptional prayers in the reformed rite are some of the sequences, *Veni sancte Spiritus* for example, but, again, these now make such rare appearances that it is best to think of them as verbal banners for their festivals rather than as normal parts of the liturgy. There was one other exception in the pre-1970 rite, the *Suscipe sancta Trinitas* at the Offertory, but its affront to the fundamental structure of euchological prayer was so gross that it was suppressed. The very action of suppressing this prayer, an innovation from around the late tenth century,[20] draws attention to the fact that Christian prayer is only possible when we pray in Christ to the Father.[21] In effect, this handful of exceptions serves to emphasise that there is a correct form for liturgical prayer, while reminding us that, in the ups-and-downs of actual worship, we have not always adhered to this format and its theological vision.

OBJECT LESSONS

Reflecting on the nature of the liturgical prayers brings about a deeper appreciation of the inter-relationship of the Christian mystery and the liturgy, but it should also remind us how we can easily misconstrue the liturgy and, as has so often happened, have it convey a false sense of what we are doing when we gather as the community of the baptised. Flowing directly from the nature of liturgical prayer we can observe how there are many common expressions that are simply out of harmony with the liturgy's inner rationale. In noting these incongruities we can delve deeper into the structure of the prayers.

Clearly, the most important consequence of seeing prayer as directed in the Christ, while offering thanks for the Christ, to the

---

20. Jungmann, *op. cit.*, vol. 2, 46-48.

21. Some Catholics who, following a recent trend, find 'ever greater riches' in the pre-1970 rite, should note this prayer carefully before going any further with the praise of a rite that had become encrusted with time's chance accretions, and ask themselves: (1) who could possibly be making this prayer in the liturgy, and (2) 'where' within a created cosmos might one be 'standing' such that one could address the Trinity collectively?

Father is that to consider the institution narrative – conceived of as 'the formula of consecration' – as a 'stand alone' prayer is wholly wide of the mark and flows from a notion of the Eucharistic Prayer not as 'Eucharistic' but as a means to producing a sacral product. This approach to the prayer has been far more prevalent in Catholic history than it is comfortable to remember; and it is still perpetuated in common parlance, in outdated rituals such as ringing bells at the elevations, and in the notion that the 'sacrament is confected'.[22] Concern that the Eucharistic Prayer might be viewed as focused on confecting the presence of the Christ may seem outmoded: surely in our liturgy, where it is clearly expressed in the vernacular that this is a prayer to the Father, such notions cannot survive! However, the understanding of the liturgy tends to operate in parallel to the actual event, and acclamations such as 'My Lord and my God' or 'Come let us worship him' destroy at one stroke the understanding not just of the Eucharistic Prayer, but of the whole gathering as a sacrifice of praise to the Father. Likewise, we tend to define Eucharistic Prayers functionally – they are to do a task and if that task is done, then it is a 'Eucharistic Prayer'. But we should rather view them in terms of the act of the whole Christ blessing the Father in an actual community meal which is the anticipation of the eschatological banquet: it is on this basis that we can see that the Anaphora of Addai and Mari is a true prayer,[23] and that there is nothing lacking in that which is found in the *Didachê*.[24]

THE PRAYER OF THE FAITHFUL

The Prayer of the Faithful, in actual current practice, often provides the clearest evidence of how little presidents have taken on board the liturgy of 1970 or the liturgical theology that underlies the renewed rite. In some places this prayer – when not omitted –

22. The very fact that Canon 927 (C.I.C. 1983) can declare it 'absolutely wrong' to confect one species outside a celebration of the Mass implicitly declares that the 'formula' is an absolute function, and that the Eucharist's 'products' could exist outside of the Christ's action of blessing the Father. This survival of a defective understanding of the event of the Eucharist is a symptom of how little many theologians have appreciated the renewal of theology sanctioned by Vatican II.

23. *Cf* R. Taft, 'Mass without the Consecration?' *America* 12 May 2003.

24. *Cf* L. Ligier, 'The Origins of the Eucharistic Prayer,' *Studia Liturgica* 9 (1973) 161-85.

can be replaced by either a set of 'novena prayers' in one place or by a time for 'shared prayer'/random 'intentions' in another community, while few seem to note the inappropriateness of including a formal prayer to Mary.[25] The art of praying this Prayer as a priestly people is one that we are only learning very slowly. This failure is partly a matter of ritual awareness and style, but it is also a lack of appreciation that the whole community celebrates the Eucharist as a priestly people with a presbyter as president of the Assembly of the New Israel.

ACTION AND IDENTIFICATION

Liturgical prayer is not a matter of words, it is the activity of the communion of the Church expressing itself in union with the Christ in his blessing of the Father, and this activity becomes a fully human act for us in our words which are at once an interpersonal act – we address the Father – and an act of recollection of who we are and how we have come to be what we are. The liturgy's prayers are, therefore, more than simply songs of praise: they unite us with our Lord, they give an expression to his act of blessing such that we can identify with it, and they tell us who we are. The prayers taken as a whole are a declaration of the Church's identity as the new priestly People of God who come together and act in union with Jesus, the child (*pais*) of the Father.

---

25. See T. O'Loughlin, 'Prayers of the Faithful: Some Notes on their Theology and Form' in *Liturgical Resources for Lent and Eastertide*, Dublin 2004, 41-44.

CHAPTER TEN

Invoking the Holy Spirit, and Remembering the Paschal Mystery

DANIEL J. HARRINGTON SJ

IT IS A GREAT PRIVILEGE for me to contribute to this volume honouring Wilfrid J. Harrington. Not only do we share the same surname, but we both have roots in the Beara Peninsula in West Cork, one of the most beautiful places on earth and the home of many named Harrington. My father was born just a few villages from where Wilfrid was born.

We share a vocation as Catholic biblical scholars committed to making available to God's people the best in contemporary biblical scholarship, and thus to help our theology and Church become more explicitly and profoundly biblical. In my own endeavors along this line, Wilfrid's work has always stood out as an excellent example to be imitated in both style and content. It is learned, personally engaged, clearly and concisely stated, as well as being positive and constructive.

My assigned topic concerns two elements found in the Church's Eucharistic Prayers (also known as *anaphoras*): *epiclêsis* (invocation) and *anamnêsis* (remembrance, memorial). I will first explain briefly the meaning of the two terms, say something about their history, and note their place in the Eucharistic Prayers used in Roman Catholic Eucharistic liturgies today. Then I will explore at more length some of the biblical roots of these two themes – invoking the Holy Spirit, and remembering the Paschal Mystery – as central to both the Christian Scriptures and the celebration of the Church's Eucharist.

EPICLÊSIS AND *ANAMNÊSIS* IN THE EUCHARISTIC LITURGY

Epiclêsis in Greek refers to a 'calling upon' or 'invocation'.[1] In the oldest extant complete Eucharistic Prayer, attributed to Hippolytus (early 3rd century), there is a prayer after the words of institution and the oblation/offering that God might 'send your Holy Spirit on the offering of your holy Church to bring together in unity all those who receive it' (that is, the Eucharistic elements). Throughout the centuries, however, there has developed a tendency to link the invocation of the Holy Spirit also (and more explicitly) to transforming the bread and wine into the body and blood of Christ. While the Roman Canon (Eucharistic Prayer I) has no obvious epiclesis, in the anaphoras developed in response to Vatican II the epiclesis is a prominent feature. Thus in Eucharistic Prayer II before the words of institution we ask that God will 'make holy, therefore, these gifts, we pray, by sending down your Spirit upon them like the dewfall, so that they become for us the Body and Blood of our Lord, Jesus Christ'. And after the words of institution, we 'pray that, partaking in the Body and Blood of Christ, we may be gathered into one by the Holy Spirit'. The same pattern of a double or 'split' epiclesis – the invocation of the Holy Spirit first over the Eucharistic elements and then for the unity of the people gathered in prayer – appears in Eucharistic Prayers III and IV.

The Greek *anamnêsis* means 'remembrance' or 'memorial'.[2] In the current Eucharistic Prayers the words of institution conclude with Jesus' command, 'Do this in memory of me', taken over from 1 Cor 11:24-25 and Lk 22:19. Early in the *Anaphora* of Hippolytus there is a long section in remembrance of Jesus' mission as saviour and redeemer, his identity as the Word of God, his incarnation, and his willingness to embrace suffering and death on our behalf. This memorial leads into the words of institution, which in turn lead into the oblation/offering: 'Remembering, therefore, your death and resurrection …' While Eucharistic Prayer I has several calls for God to 'remember' God's people living and dead, there is

---

1. For a concise discussion, see Frank C. Senn, "Epiclêsis," in Peter E. Fink, editor, *The New Dictionary of Sacramental Worship*, Collegeville, MN: Michael Glazier/Liturgical Press, 1990, 390-91.

2. See Senn, "Anamnêsis," *op. cit.*, 45-46.

also after the words of institution a statement about celebrating 'the memorial of Christ, your Son' and a list of what should be remembered about him: his passion, resurrection, and ascension, along with the many gifts given by God through Christ. Likewise in the other post-Vatican II anaphoras, the anamnesis has a prominent place after the words of institution: 'Therefore as we celebrate the memorial of his death and resurrection' (Eucharistic Prayer II); 'Therefore, O Lord, we celebrate the memorial of the saving Passion of your Son' (III); and 'Therefore, O Lord, as we now celebrate the memorial of our redemption' (IV).

EPICLÊSIS: INVOKING THE HOLY SPIRIT

The biblical words for 'spirit' present problems for translators. The Hebrew *ruah* is a feminine noun that can mean 'breath', 'wind', or 'spirit' in the sense of what makes a human person alive. In the Old Testament one must analyse each instance and try to determine what meaning best suits the context. The Greek *pneuma* is a neuter noun and displays the same ambiguity ('breath', 'wind', or 'spirit') as the Hebrew word does. Moreover, *pneuma* can be used, especially by Paul, in the anthropological sense of a faculty or disposition alongside the flesh (*sarx*) and the soul (*psychê*). It is that aspect of persons that allows them to be open to the promptings of the Holy Spirit. And of course, *pneuma* is also the Greek word used in the New Testament and in other early Christian writings to designate the Holy Spirit, the third person in the Christian doctrine of the Trinity. In Romans, Chapter 8, for example, Paul deliberately plays on the ambiguity of the word, and explores the relationship between *pneuma* in the sense of the aspect of the person that is open and responsive to God, and *pneuma* in the sense of Holy Spirit as involved in guiding and nurturing the people of God.

In invoking the 'holy spirit' (the epiclesis) at Mass we are clearly talking about the Holy Spirit, and we are calling on the Spirit to transform the bread and wine into the body and blood of Christ and to bring about greater unity among all who participate in the Eucharist. The former task can look like magic unless we situate it in the biblical perspective of the Holy Spirit's activity in creation.

When read from a Christian theological perspective, the Bible suggests that 'the spirit of God' was active in creation from the beginning and was (and is) capable of transforming chaos into order in the present and future. According to Gen 1:2, the 'ruah/pneuma of God' was hovering like a bird over the waters of chaos below. While the words *ruah* and *pneuma* can here be rendered 'wind' or 'breath' (as most modern translations do), a theological case can also be (and has been) made for 'the spirit of God' or even 'the (Holy) Spirit of God'.

The role of the Spirit/spirit of God in creation hinted at in Gen 1:2 is developed especially in the Book of Wisdom/Wisdom of Solomon, a first-century BCE Jewish book about wisdom, written in Greek, in Alexandria. The author describes 'the spirit of the Lord' as that which 'has filled the world, and that which holds all things together' (Wis 1:7). Some scholars have compared this concept to the Stoic philosophical idea of a 'world soul' that animates and preserves all living creatures. In 7:22-23 the author describes personified Wisdom, at greater length, in terms of the spirit of God:

> There is in her a spirit that is intelligent, holy, unique, manifold, subtle, mobile, clear, unpolluted, distinct, invulnerable, loving the good, keen, irresistible, beneficent, humane, steadfast, sure, free from anxiety, all-powerful, overseeing all, and penetrating through all sprits that are intelligent, pure, and altogether subtle.

The author continues the description of Wisdom/the Spirit of God as the world soul and the reflection of God's glory: 'For she is a breath of the power of God, and a pure emanation of the glory of the Almighty … a reflection of eternal light, a spotless mirror of the working of God, and an image of his goodness' (Wis 7:25-26). Some of these descriptions equally well fit Jesus as the Wisdom of God and the Son of God (see Heb 1:3). For our purposes, the point is that the first epiclesis in the Eucharistic Prayer must be read in the context of the biblical theme of the Holy Spirit as active in creation in general and thus in transforming the elements of bread and wine into the body and blood of Christ.

The invocation of the Holy Spirit to unite those persons who share in the Eucharist has an even richer biblical background. Several of the prophets (see Isa 32:15; Ezek 39:29; Zech 12:10) hope for and look forward to a dramatic future manifestation of the spirit of God being 'poured out' upon God's people. Typical of this is the hope expressed in Joel 2:28-29 (Heb. 3:1-2) in which God promises to 'pour forth my sprit on all flesh' – a prophecy regarded as having been fulfilled at Pentecost (see Acts 2:17-21). The psalm response based on Ps 104:30 used at the liturgy for Pentecost Sunday captures the hope of God's people in the Bible: 'Lord, send forth your Spirit and renew the face of earth'. In the Eucharistic liturgy we are asking God to pour forth his Holy Spirit upon us and to draw us into greater unity among ourselves and with those with whom we come into contact.

The principal New Testament writers – Luke, John and Paul – develop the theme of the activity of the Holy Spirit especially with reference to Jesus and the Church. According to Luke's infancy narrative, Jesus is to be conceived through the Holy Spirit (Lk 1:35), and Zechariah and Simeon prophesy about him under the guidance of the Holy Spirit (1:67; 2:25-35). At Jesus' baptism the Holy Spirit descends upon him (3:21-22), and his public activity of teaching and healing is empowered through the coming upon him of the Holy Spirit (4:18-19). During his public activity, and indeed during his passion, it appears that all the energies of the Holy Spirit are focused on him. And he promises to send the Spirit upon his disciples after his ascension (24:49). In the Acts of Apostles, the Holy Spirit is the principle of continuity between the time of Jesus and the Church's time. The Pentecost event (Acts 2) marks the transformation of Jesus' first followers from frightened and confused persons into fearless heralds of the good news about Jesus. Thus the Spirit empowers Peter, Paul, and other apostles, to carry on the mission of Jesus not only in their native land but even 'to the ends of the earth' (1:8).

Likewise in the Fourth Gospel, Jesus' experience of the Holy Spirit during his baptism by John (Jn 1:29-34) marks the starting point for his own public activity in which he manifests the power of the Holy Spirit as the revealer and the revelation of his Father.

At the moment of death (19:30) Jesus is said to have given up 'his spirit', surely an irony meant to describe his physical death as well as his passing on to his followers the gift of the Holy Spirit. On Easter Sunday evening the risen Jesus appears to his disciples, breathes on them and says, 'Receive the Holy Spirit' (20:22).

Through his long farewell discourse in chapters 14–17 of the Gospel according to John, Jesus had prepared his disciples (and the hearers and readers of the gospel) about what they can expect from the Holy Spirit, also known as the 'Paraclete'. That term reflects a Greek verb meaning to 'encourage, console, comfort, come to the aid of'. Today the term 'Paraclete' is translated as 'Advocate', 'Helper', or 'Comforter'. At five points Jesus clarifies the role of the Holy Spirit in carrying on the movement begun by him during his earthly ministry, and gives us a sense of the kind of unity we pray for as we invoke the Holy Spirit to come upon us and bind us into greater unity. In Jn 14:16-17 Jesus promises to send 'another Advocate', who will stand in for Jesus, guide the community of Jesus' followers in the present, and continue his work. In 14:25-26 Jesus specifies the Paraclete's role as teaching the community and reminding it of Jesus' own teachings, thus enabling his followers to face new situations while ensuring continuity with his teaching. According to 15:26-27, in the face of intense hatred from 'the world', the community will have the help of the Holy Spirit as its Advocate, who will bear witness to Jesus and enable his disciples to bear witness too. In this legal context the Paraclete serves as the defence attorney. In 16:8-11 the focus of the Paraclete's activity is with 'the world', and the Paraclete now functions more as the prosecuting attorney who will convict the world about 'sin and righteousness and judgment'. And in 16:12-15 Jesus promises that the Paraclete will extend Jesus' teaching mission by guiding the community in Jesus' way in new circumstances so as to glorify Jesus and his Father. The fidelity of the Paraclete to this mission is based on the unity that exists among Father, Son, and Holy Spirit.

If Luke and John give us rich theological resources for what we can expect when we call upon the Holy Spirit, Paul's letters provide us with theology tested in the fire of experience. Paul's letters were occasional communications from the apostle in response to pastoral problems that had arisen in his absence, and Paul is best understood as a pastoral theologian. It has been said that if you wish to understand the crises in our Church today, read Paul's First Letter to the Corinthians. There you will find factions in the Christian community, sexual immorality, lawsuits between Christians, debates about the relative value of marriage and celibacy, clashes between the 'strong' and the 'weak', socioeconomic and liturgical abuses at the Eucharist and community assemblies, the relative importance of speaking in tongues, doubts about the resurrection, and conflicts over the money given at the Sunday collection.

In response to these many problems, in Chapters 12, 13 and 14 Paul urges the Corinthian Christians to look upon their community as being under the active guidance of the Holy Spirit and to regard themselves as individually gifted by the Holy Spirit: 'To each is given the manifestation of the Spirit for the common good' (12:7). Their special spiritual gifts (*pneumatika*) originate with the Spirit (*pneuma*). They differ among themselves, and they are to be used in concert for building up the body of Christ. Their exercise must be carried out in a spirit of love: 'Love is patient; love is kind; love is not envious ...' (13:4-7). The relative value of these spiritual gifts is best measured not by their spectacular manifestations (like speaking in tongues) but rather by the extent to which they benefit others and the community as a whole. Thus the Holy Spirit is the principle and source of unity within the Christian community. This is what we pray for when invoking the Holy Spirit (*epiclêsis*) in our Eucharistic Prayers today.

ANAMNÊSIS: REMEMBERING THE PASCHAL MYSTERY

When we remember some person, place or event, we bring them to mind again. Our memories of them may be pleasant or not, but in any case they have an effect on us in the present time. What we remember especially in the anamnesis present in our Eucharistic Prayers today is the Christ-event or Paschal Mystery, that is, Jesus' death and resurrection and its saving significance. The early Anaphora of Hippolytus provides a much wider lens on the person and mission of Jesus, including his pre-existence as the Word of God and his incarnation.

One of my teachers, G. Ernest Wright, used to describe the Old Testament as 'The Book of the Mighty Acts of God (*magnalia Dei*)'.[3] He regarded the Torah, the Historical Books and the Prophets (the Wisdom books never fit very well) as constituting the ancient Israelites' memory of how God had acted in their history. The two most important of God's mighty acts were the creation of the world and enabling the people's exodus from slavery in Egypt. The psalmists and the prophets often pointed to these two mighty acts as good reasons for trusting in God's promises in their own time. Thus the prophet responsible for Isaiah 40–55 (Second Isaiah) sought to persuade those Jews living in Babylon in the 6th century BCE to return home to Jerusalem by portraying the 'new thing' God was doing in terms of a new creation and a new exodus. In the same vein, those offering sacrifices in the Land of Israel were instructed in Deut 26:5-9 to recite what seems to have been a very early confession of faith about the mighty acts of God from Abraham through the exodus to the people's entrance into the Promised Land.

A very important dimension of the biblical concept of 'remembrance' appears in the Book of Deuteronomy. Cast in the form of Moses' farewell discourses to the people who are about to enter the Promised Land, Deuteronomy was written much later (probably in the 6th century BCE). Nevertheless, in introducing the Ten Commandments, 'Moses' insists that

> ... not with our ancestors did the Lord make this covenant, but with us, who are all of us here alive today. The Lord spoke with you face to face at the mountain, out of the fire (5:3-4; see 29:10,12).

The idea is that by remembering the great events of the past (in this case, the giving of the Law at Horeb/Sinai) it is possible for those calling them to mind now really to participate in them. The past becomes the present, and the present becomes the past. Likewise, Jews who celebrate Passover today are urged to regard themselves as truly present in the events connected with ancient Israel's escape from slavery in Egypt and being recited as part of the Passover Haggadah. Likewise also, as at Mass we remember

---

3. Wright, *The Book of the Acts of God*, Garden City, NY, Doubleday, 1960.

Jesus' death and resurrection, we can and should regard ourselves as mystically present at Jesus' Last Supper as we fulfill his command to 'do this in memory of me' (1 Cor 11:25; Lk 22:19).

The Gospels constitute the major evidence for the early Christians' remembrances of Jesus. Having passed through a complex process of composition, these texts now provide the material for our own remembrances of Jesus.[4] Martin Kähler's famous description of Mark's Gospel as a passion narrative with a long introduction applies to all four canonical Gospels and highlights the climactic place of the passion narratives within them. While describing Jesus in his own time (around 30 BCE) and place (Palestine), they were written in such a way that we too can participate in them, at least by means of our imagination. The institution of the Eucharist takes place in the context of Jesus' passion and death, and that is one reason why our liturgical anamnesis focuses on Jesus' death and resurrection.

Another reason is that many of the earliest summaries of Christian faith highlight the importance of Jesus' death and resurrection. For example, in 1 Cor 15:3b-5, Paul quotes the message that he himself received and then handed on to the Corinthian Christians: 'that Christ died for our sins in accordance with the scriptures, and that he was buried, and that he was raised on the third day in accordance with the scriptures, and that he appeared to Cephas, then to the twelve'. (For similar statements of early Christian faith that focus on Jesus' death and resurrection, see Rom 3:25; 1 Tim 1:5; 2:5-6; 3:16; and 2 Tim 2:11-13.)

Writing to the Romans, Paul's primary concern is with the results or effects for us of Jesus' death and resurrection. Paul was convinced that all persons – Gentiles and Jews alike – stood in need of the revelation of God's righteousness (covenant fidelity) through Jesus. He regarded humankind before and apart from Christ as being in slavery to three evil powers – Sin, Death and the Law. Furthermore, he believed that through his death and resurrection Jesus had

---

4. James D. G. Dunn, in his book *Jesus Remembered* (Grand Rapids and Cambridge, Eerdmans, 2003), contends that the Jesus tradition is Jesus remembered, and that the Jesus thus remembered is as close as we will ever be able to reach back to the historical Jesus.

overcome those powers and made possible a new and better relationship with God. The great themes of Pauline theology – justification, faith, redemption, reconciliation, sanctification, access to God, salvation, grace, peace with God, glorification, and so on – these were some of Paul's ways of talking about what God had done for us in and through Christ. Paul's Letter to the Romans was his vehicle for reminding the Christians there to stop quarrelling along the lines of ethnic identity (Jews versus Gentiles), and to recognize and act upon the unity they had received in and through Christ. Of course, this is the reason for the presence of the *anamnêsis* of the Paschal Mystery in our Eucharistic Prayers. It reminds us of the pivotal significance of Jesus' (past) death and resurrection for us in the present.

The Letter to the Hebrews represents still another approach to the Paschal Mystery. Best understood as a sermon in written form, Hebrews in 4:14–10:18 provides an extended reflection on Jesus' passion and death in terms of what the Old Testament says about sacrifice and priesthood. Its basic theological point is that Christ is both the perfect sacrifice for sins (perfect in the sense of truly effective) and the great high priest who offered himself willingly as the sacrifice for sins.

Hebrews seems to have been written for early Christians (perhaps at Rome) who were experiencing spiritual weariness and discouragement. As Thomas G. Long has noted, what is most remarkable is the preacher's conviction that this state of spiritual exhaustion was best met by Christology and by preaching. The author's solution was not improved group dynamics, conflict management techniques, or more lively liturgies (however valuable these may be!). Rather, he was bold enough to preach to his congregation 'in complex theological terms about the nature and meaning of Jesus Christ'.[5] Perhaps the Catholic church in Ireland and in the USA (and elsewhere) can learn an important lesson from the author of Hebrews and from the foundational biblical-pastoral work of Wilfrid J. Harrington OP.

---

5. Long, *Hebrews Interpretation*, Louisville: John Knox Press, 1997, 3, 5.

CHAPTER ELEVEN

The Glory of the Lord

SEÁN FREYNE

DOXOLOGIES were a very important element in early Christian worship and prayer life, as a hymnic form of prayer of praise to God. They reflect the sense of joyful celebration that is the hallmark of the earliest proclamations of the good news. Paul in particular repeatedly breaks into this form of refrain as he seeks to expound the meaning of his gospel to various audiences (Gal 1:5; Rom 11:36; 16:27; Eph 3:21; 1 Tim 1:17; 6:15-16). But doxologies are characteristic of other branches of the movement also, and are attested regularly in second century literature: *e.g.* 1 Pet 4:11; Jude 25; *Didachê* IX,2.4; 10,2; *1 Clement* 45,7; 64,2; *Mart. Pol.* 20,2; 22,1.[1]

Somewhat later, when the Christological debates were raging, the precise formulation of the Christian doxology took on a new significance, especially in the West during the Arian controversy. Initially the offering of praise was directed to the Father through the Son. However, gradually the Son also became the object of such worship, and after the Council of Nicea, which defined the Trinitarian understanding of God, what came to be known as the 'lesser doxology' ('Glory be to the Father and to the Son and to the Holy Spirit', etc.) canonized this formulation, itself based on the early baptismal formula of Mt 28:18. Even then the second part of the doxology – 'as it was in the beginning, is now and ever shall be, world without end, Amen' – was the subject of some controversy: to what precisely does the 'it' (Latin: *sicut erat in principio*) refer? While it is customary today to take it to mean the

---

1. D. Aune, 'Worship, Early Christian,' *Anchor Bible Dictionary* (6 vols. ed. D.N. Freedman, New York: Doubleday, 1992), vol. 6, 973-989, especially 981f.

divine glory (*kabod*) as reflected in creation, for a considerable period in the West at least, it was taken to refer to the Son's eternal existence as the Logos, alluding to Jn 1:1.[2]

THE GLORY OF THE LORD IN THE HEBREW SCRIPTURES

Leaving these Christological debates to one side for now, a prior question has to do with the origins of the doxology as a prayer form. In fact we do not have to go very far for our answer. Both the Hebrew Scriptures (the Christian Old Testament) and later Jewish writings provide ample evidence that this form of address to God was commonplace in the prayer of Israel and continued on in later Judaism also.[3] As such Paul's frequent use of the form is a pointer to his own Jewish upbringing and background. An early Israelite canticle in the Book of Deuteronomy recounts all that God did for Israel in the past. The author begins by declaring: 'I will proclaim the name of the Lord, ascribe greatness to our God' (Dt 32:3). The canticle goes on to describe God's relationship with his people in the most intimate terms: he is the Rock, his works are perfect and all his ways are just; he is the Father who created them and who protected them in the desert 'like an eagle that stirs up its nest and flutters over its young, spreading out its wings, catching them, bearing them on its pinions' (vv. 6,11). It is this sense of God's constant care for Israel throughout its troubled history that was to inspire later psalmists and prophets to continue to develop the literary form of the doxology as one of the most appropriate forms for addressing God.

A paradoxical aspect of the Israelite experience of God is the sense of God's nearness, and yet God's hiddenness. The incident with Moses at the burning bush sets the tone: Moses asks for God's name, only to be given a promise – 'I will be the one who will be with you', but no name is given (Ex 3:14). This response is not intended to make a philosophical statement about God's nature as suggested by the later LXX translation *egô eimi ho ôn* ('I am who

---

2. J.R. Sachs, 'Glory,' *The New Dictionary of Theology*, ed. J. A. Komonchak, M. Collins and D.A. Lane, Dublin: Gill and Macmillan, 1987, 417-20.
3. M. Daly-Denton, *Psalm-shaped Prayerfulness. A Guide to the Christian Reception of the Psalms*, Dublin: Columba Press, 2010, 114-27.

am'). Rather it identifies the name with God's free and sovereign action in history, and it is only by contemplating this action that God's name begins to take on real content and meaning. Subsequently, when Moses asks to see God's glory he is told he cannot see God's face and live. However, God will make his goodness pass before him and proclaim his name. Moses must hide in a cleft of the rock and God will cover his face with his hand while the glory passes by (Ex 33:17-23).[4]

This delightful vignette tells us much about Israel's theodicy. Glory, name, face: these are all aspects of the divine, which humans experience as goodness. Yet there is a gulf between the human and the divine, and that dividing line must be clearly marked, no matter how much God can and must be portrayed in anthropological terms. Arising from this fundamental aspect of Israel's theodicy, a serious problem was posed, namely, how to continue to speak of God's nearness, while also maintaining respect for the mysterious nature of God. The outcome was the development of a number of epithets for God, describing him in human terms with regard to his actions on behalf of Israel: warrior, healer, judge, teacher, shepherd, redeemer, etc.

However, particularly after the Babylonian exile, when some at least were beginning to question the idea of God's constancy on behalf of his people, a sense of God's distance began to emerge, even as the Lord God was given more universal traits as creator and sustainer of the whole universe, a global rather than merely a tribal God. Various ways were found to bridge the emerging gap between the human and divine worlds, including the postulation of intermediate beings, God's *malakim* or messengers/angels. This development also gave rise to the image of God surrounded by his heavenly hosts, so that he can be described as 'Lord God Sabaoth', 'Lord of hosts/armies'. In a similar manner, even though Moses' request for revelation of the name of this liberating God was refused, the notion of the name (*shem*) rather than God's self, emerges as an important way of reassuring Israel that it had not

---

4. G. von Rad, *Old Testament Theology*, 2 vols. (trans. D.M.G. Stalker) Edinburgh and London: Oliver and Boyd, 1963, vol. 1, 179-87.

been abandoned. The name took on an objective existence of its own, though always with a clear awareness of the initial promise and refusal to disclose its content fully. Thus, for instance, God has made his name to dwell in the temple in Jerusalem where all Israel was to gather (Deut 16:2). Psalmists repeatedly speak of honouring God's name, to the extent that the very word had come to represent God's self, but without attempting to unveil the mystery that was that self.

The notion of God's glory should be understood in this context of tension between presence and absence of the Deity. Indeed 'glory' appears to be the most complete expression of God's self in the Israelite theological vocabulary. This emerges in the account of Moses' encounter at the rock, just discussed. Moses desires to see God's glory, but the response is that God will make his goodness pass before him – even proclaim his name – but neither Moses, nor indeed any human can see the glory and live. Reading this text one has a sense of a liturgical occasion in the Jerusalem temple of later times being projected back onto the founding desert experience. God's deeds are recounted and his name proclaimed, yet the veil behind which God's glory resides remains in place, as a hidden presence. The first verse of Psalm 19 expresses this role of the *Kabod Yahweh* perfectly by distinguishing between the heavens and the firmament beneath the heavens of the creation story: 'The heavens are telling the glory of God, and the firmament proclaims his handiwork.' God's glory resides in heaven properly even when its effects are experienced on earth. This aspect is developed further in visionary writings of a later date, as we shall see.

The pre-eminence of the term glory (*kabod*) among the Hebrew epithets for God has given rise to the notion of the doxology as a central dimension of human recognition of the divine. The Hebrew term *kabod* is almost invariably translated in the LXX by *doxa*. These terms have not dissimilar everyday meanings that carry over in interesting ways to their theological usage. *Kabod* had the ordinary sense of honour, but this was seen in practical terms as 'weightiness' or 'importance'. Thus the term can be used figuratively to refer to what is deemed to be impressive, demanding recognition. It is in this sense that it is used repeatedly for God's presence with and activity for Israel that is to be acknowledged and celebrated. Likewise with *doxa*: its root meaning is 'appearance' or 'opinion'. However, in the LXX translation of the Bible it invariably takes on the biblical rather than the secular Greek significance, being used to translate *kabod* 180 times. It thus assumes the character of a technical term, emphasizing reality over appearance, and bestowing on the term 'doxology' a definite theological and liturgical significance.[5]

It is worth tracing briefly the contours of the use of *kabod* in relation to God within different strands of the Biblical tradition. Significantly, in many early contexts the *Kabod Yahweh* is associated with such natural phenomena as thunderstorms, lightning and other major disturbances in the physical universe. Here we can see a suggestion of the root meaning of that which causes an impression on humans. However, the association goes deeper and is based on the widely diffused idea in the Hebrew Bible that, as the Creator, God can and does manifest himself through natural phenomena. Not that the Lord God was ever seen merely as a God of Thunder like the Greek Zeus, for example.

Particularly in the Psalms one finds echoes of the creation narrative in the repeated enumeration of all the elements of the created cosmos – the heavens and the heavenly bodies, the waters of the deep, the earth and its creatures, including humans – being summoned to celebrate the glory of God (*eg*, Pss 24; 29; 148). Inevitably, God's glory is associated with the revelation at Sinai also, when God descends on Mount Sinai in a thick cloud, with thunder and lightning (Ex 19:16,18; 24:15ff).

As already suggested, the manifestations of the *Kabod Yahweh* take on an other-worldly dimension in terms of out-of-the-ordinary experiences in the natural world: thunder and lightning storms, earthquakes, and the like. Yet the narratives seem to reflect the liturgical activity of the Jerusalem temple as this can be reconstructed from our sources. Psalm 24 in particular gives us a glimpse of the pious Israelites pondering on their worthiness to

---

5. G. Kittel and G. von Rad, article 'Doxa' in *Theological Dictionary of the New Testament* (tr. G. Bromiley), Grand Rapids MI, Eerdmans, 1964-), vol. 2, 233-47.

enter the temple in order 'to see the face of the God of Jacob.' Buoyed by a sense of expectation and joy, the Psalmist imagines a procession in which the King of glory enters:

> Lift up your heads, O gates! And be lifted up, O ancient doors!
> that the King of glory may come in! Who is the King of glory?
> The Lord strong and mighty, the Lord mighty in battle!
> Lift up your heads, O gates! And be lifted up O ancient doors!
> That the king of glory may come in. Who is the King of glory?
> The Lord of hosts, he is the King of Glory (Ps 24:7-9).

The author of the Priestly Document – one of the four putative sources of the Pentateuch – projects this idea of God manifesting himself at certain times and places, back to the desert days of Israel's wanderings. 'The tent of meeting' is the place where the glory of the Lord could be encountered, thereby suggesting divine mobility, but also God's special presence within Israel. Significantly, however, a distinction is made between the cloud that covers the tent and the glory that fills the tent. The cloud is, therefore, merely a sign of the divine presence, and when it was there Moses could not enter, 'because the glory of the Lord filled the tent'. Here the glory is deemed to be a radiant, fiery substance (Ex 40:34-35).

Solomon's building of a central sanctuary somewhat altered this understanding of the manner in which the divine presence was understood, centralizing it in one place (1 Kgs 8:22-30). This was further emphasized in the Deuteronomic reforms of the seventh century (Deut 16). Now the *Kabod Yahweh* is deemed to be present behind the veil of the tabernacle, seated on a throne placed on the Ark of the Covenant in the inner sanctum, surrounded by the heavenly beings, the cherubim and seraphim. This link between the *Kabod Yahweh* and the temple is particularly developed by the great Jerusalem prophets Isaiah and Ezechiel.

Isaiah's prophetic call takes place within the temple with his famous vision of the heavenly throne:

> In the year that king Uzziah died, I saw the Lord sitting on a throne, high and lifted up; and his train filled the temple. Above him stood the seraphim; each had six wings; with two he covered his face, and with two he covered his feet and with

two he flew. And one called to the other and said: 'Holy, Holy, Holy, is the Lord of hosts; the whole earth is full of his glory'. And the foundations of the thresholds shook at the voice of him who called and the house was filled with smoke. And I said: 'Woe is me! For I am lost; for I am a man of unclean lips, and I dwell in the midst of people of unclean lips. For my eyes have seen the King the Lord of hosts!' (Isa 6:1-5).

At first reading this scene is quite remarkable in that Isaiah, unlike Moses, is given a glimpse of the Lord God seated on his throne. Yet, as von Rad notes, the purpose of the vision is not to reveal the inner nature of Israel's God, but rather to make the prophet conscious of his own and Israel's unworthiness, when confronted with the holiness of God. Indeed, it is the doxology of the Seraphim, the Trishagion ('The Thrice-Holy One') that acts as the interpretative prompt for the prophet to realize the distance between the human and the divine, even though the *Kabod Yahweh* fills the whole earth, if only Israel had eyes to see.[6]

Two centuries later another Jerusalemite, Ezechiel, had a similar experience, not however in the temple, since it was in ruins, but rather among the exiles in Babylon. Once again, the vision is aimed at the commissioning of the prophet, set against the background of Israel's continuing sinfulness and its impending destruction. The prophet's initial vision is described much more elaborately than that of Isaiah, especially the details regarding the winged creatures, half human, half animal, who draw God's chariot (Ezek 1:4-24). The divine reality is described in terms of the traditional cosmic features of the theophany: clouds, light, and fire. The actual theophany is described in terms not dissimilar to that of Isaiah:

And above the firmament, over their heads there was the likeness of a throne, in appearance like sapphire, and seated above the likeness of a throne was a likeness as it were of a human form. And upwards from what had the appearance of his loins, I saw as it were gleaming bronze, like fire enclosed round about; and downwards from what had the appearance of his loins, I saw as it were the appearance of fire, and there

6. G. von Rad, *Old Testament Theology*, vol.2, 53-63.

was brightness round about it. Like the appearance of the bow that is in the cloud on the day of rain, so was the appearance of the brightness round about. Such was the appearance of the brightness of the glory of the Lord (Ezek 1:26-28).

There is a palpable hesitancy to this description with the frequent use of words such as 'appearance,' 'likeness,' and 'as it were'. Unlike Isaiah's vision earlier there is no heavenly doxology, but rather a sense of strangeness and distance of the divine presence, still described in terms of the *kabod*. Perhaps the reason for these features of the narrative has to do with the fact that the author is already away from Jerusalem with the exiles (Ezek 1:1-3). Somewhat later we hear of another vision of the prophet, this time transposed briefly back to Jerusalem, there to witness the departure of the *kabod* from the temple and the city. There is a slight hint of hope as the prophet sees the *kabod* hovering over Jerusalem, before departing for the east – presumably to be with the exiles in Babylon (Ezek 10:18-22). This note is taken up in the vision of restoration that is the new temple where the *kabod* returns to take up residence once more in Jerusalem:[7]

Behold the glory of the God of Israel came from the east, and the sound of his coming was like the sound of many waters. And the earth shone with his glory. And the vision I saw was like the vision which I had seen when he came to destroy the city and like the vision I had seen beside the river Chebar. And I fell upon my face. As the glory of the Lord arrived at the temple by the east gate, the Spirit lifted me up and brought me into the inner court; I saw the glory of the Lord filled the temple … I heard one speaking to me out of the temple, and he said to me: Son of Man this is the place of my throne and the place of the soles of my feet, where I will dwell among the people of Israel forever (Ezek 43:2-7).

Before turning to the development of the doxological tradition in the New Testament, it is important to pause and note some insights from our survey thus far. This was the tradition of worship and spirituality that all branches of Early Christianity were heir to:

7. *Ibid*, 220-37.

1) Despite the use of many and various epithets for God, the emergence of 'glory' as the most appropriate one for expressing Israel's experience of the divine, indicates that the People gave expression to a sense of awe and delight at God's benevolence, but also to a recognition of God's power, majesty and otherness.

2) Attendant images such as 'throne', 'hosts', 'servants', 'messengers' evoke the world of ancient Near Eastern Kingship. While drawing freely on this field of imagery, Israel never forgot her experience of God's *hesed*, *emeth* and *sedaqah*, that is, God's loving kindness, faithfulness and saving justice that differentiated him from all earthly kings.

3) The fact that the Temple came to be associated with the *Kabod Yahweh*, as in the case of Isaiah and Ezechiel, meant that a sense of communal celebration of the divine presence was central to Israel's life in the land.

4) Despite this development, the Psalmists never allowed the memory of God's presence in the wilderness to be forgotten. God's 'glory' infused the whole of God's creation, since the heavens were his throne and the earth his footstool. 'Giving glory to God' or 'Blessing his name' could only be understood as calls to recognize the true nature of the God who had graciously visited them.

CHRISTOLOGY AS SOURCE FOR DOXOLOGY
IN EARLY CHRISTIANITY

Writing to the emperor Trajan in c. 112 CE, Pliny, governor of the Roman province of Bithynia, described Christian practices in his province. Among other things he mentions that at their communal meetings they 'sang hymns (*carmen dicere*) to Christ as a God'. Much earlier Paul, or his disciple, encourages his Colossian converts to continue to sing prayers, hymns and spiritual canticles, but without mentioning whether this was to God or to Christ (3:16). Larry Hurtado has argued persuasively that it was in the context of Christian worship that the first followers of Jesus began to ascribe divine status to him.[8] One would imagine that this development

---

8. L. Hurtado, *Lord Jesus Christ. Devotion to Jesus in Earliest Christianity*, Grand Rapids, MI, Eerdmans, esp. 134-54.

had begun among the Hellenistic converts, since the practice of acknowledging certain heroic figures such as Hercules, Dionysus and Isis was widespread in Greco-Roman antiquity.

Strict Jewish monotheism, it is claimed, would have inhibited people of Jewish background making such claims for Jesus. The messiah was not deemed to be a god, even though in later Judaism certain figures such as the heavenly Son of Man (Dn 7) or Lady Wisdom (Prov 8) could be described as having divine agency in the world together with the Lord God. In discussing the issue of idol worship, Paul, writing c. 50 CE, reminds his Corinthian audience that their belief, derived from the great Jewish *Shema* prayer (Deut 6:4ff), differs from that of their pagan neighbours:

> We know that an idol has no real existence and that there 'is no God but one'. For although there may be so-called gods in heaven or in earth – as indeed there are many 'gods' and many 'lords' – yet for us there is one God, the Father, from whom are all things and for whom we exist, and one Lord, Jesus Christ, through whom are all things and through whom we exist (1 Cor 8:4-6).

Even at that early stage of development Paul is still able to appeal to what we may call a Christianized version of Jewish monotheistic belief, giving God the epithet 'Father' (echoing Jesus' use of *Abba* as an address for God) and transposing the title 'Lord' (*Kyrios*, the LXX term for *Yahweh*) to Jesus. God, the Father's role as source (*ek*) and end (*eis*) of all created reality is acknowledged, but Jesus is now ascribed the title *Kyrios* and his role as instrumental cause (*dia*) highlighted. Difference of roles need not imply inferiority of persons, even as the historical pattern of creation and redemption is acknowledged in this example of early Christian theologizing.

Such development in Christological thinking undoubtedly played an important role in the production of early Christian doxologies. Again Paul is our earliest witness to the process. In another early Christian hymn which he cites, the injunction is that 'every knee should bend, and every tongue confess, that Jesus Christ is Lord, to the glory (*eis doxan*) of God the Father' (Phil 2:6-11). The bending of the knee and confessing by the tongue clearly signal a setting of celebration and worship. The new status of Jesus was not something that he himself achieved. Rather it was achieved through the *Kabod Yahweh*, present and active in the world generally, and manifested particularly in the life, death and resurrection of Jesus of Nazareth.

That Paul, and other early Christian teachers and preachers, were deeply influenced by the *Kabod Yahweh* tradition emerges from another Pauline text, Second Corinthians. In a polemical argument against his Judaizing opponents in Corinth, Paul draws a negative comparison between the old and new dispensations, contrasting the incident of Moses having to cover his face lest he see the passing glory of God (Ex 34:29-35), with the free access to that glory that is available in the new dispensation through Jesus Christ (2 Cor 3). He acknowledges that the original dispensation was indeed given in glory (v. 9), but he interprets the covering of the face negatively, taking it as symbolic of continuing Jewish blindness to the 'dispensation of righteousness'. As a result 'that which once had glory' no longer has it, 'because of the glory that surpasses it'. By contrast those of the new dispensation who have received the Spirit, and with it freedom, are able with unveiled face to behold the glory of the Lord, 'being changed into his likeness from one degree of glory to another'. The image of the divine glory, so circumscribed in the Hebrew Bible out of a sense of reverence for the Godhead, can now become the metaphor for humanity's transformation, achieved in the Christ event. Far from rejecting his Jewish heritage, therefore, Paul – in a polemical situation to be sure – is drawing on that heritage to suggest its final realization in Christ.

For Paul, then, *doxa* expresses the condition of the risen Christ, by the glory of the Father. He can declare 'The Lord (i.e. Jesus) is the Spirit', meaning that in his transformed state Jesus now shares the being of God's self. Since in Paul's thought Jesus has attained this status as redeemer of humanity, believers, who previously had 'fallen short of the glory of God', can also now participate in it (cf Rom 3:21-26). This saving event is best described as a new creation:

> For it is the God who said 'Let light shine out of darkness who has shone in our hearts to give the light of the knowledge of the glory of God in the face of Christ (2 Cor 4:6; *cf* Rom 8:18-25).

In contrast to the Pauline emphasis, the Synoptic Gospels, though written from a post-Resurrection perspective also, are quite reserved in applying *doxa* to Jesus in their accounts of his earthly life, as distinct from his second coming. Thus, for instance, both Mark and Matthew, while describing the Transfiguration story in theophanic colours, do not use the term 'glory' in describing Jesus' altered state (Mk 9:2-8; Mt 17:1-8), but they do speak of him as the future Son of Man coming 'in the glory of his Father' (Mk 8:38; Mt 16:27; 19:28; 24:30; 25:31).

Luke, however, is somewhat more daring, describing both Moses and Elijah 'appearing in glory', a condition shared by Jesus also at the Transfiguration (Lk 9:28-36). Indeed the third Evangelist brackets the whole story of Jesus in terms of the glory of the Lord. Thus we hear that the glory of the Lord shone around the shepherds as they received the good news of salvation in the beginning. Shortly afterwards they hear the whole heavenly host singing 'Glory to God in the highest and peace to his people on earth', a song of praise that would serve as the opening lines of the 'great doxology', the *Gloria in excelsis Deo*, which was developed later (Lk 2:9,14,32). At the close of the gospel the risen Jesus explains to the two baffled disciples in Emmaus: 'Ought not Christ to have suffered these things and so enter his glory?' (Lk 24:26). Perhaps Luke's usage was determined somewhat by his Greco-Roman audience, who would have expected that Jesus should be a glorious figure, if indeed he was to challenge the political might of Rome, as Luke's story claims.[9]

Finally, the Johannine use of the term 'glory' as applied to Jesus is highly developed, beginning with the programmatic declaration of the Prologue: 'And the Word became flesh and dwelt amongst us, and we have seen his glory, the glory as it were of the only begotten with the Father, full of grace and truth' (Jn 1:14). The author of the Fourth Gospel is quite familiar with the ordinary meanings of the term – 'reputation', 'respect', 'opinion', 'honour' – and he can bring these into play through the literary device of

9. Cf. F. Bovon, *Luke 1* (Hermeneia Commentary Series), Minneapolis, MN: Augsburg, Fortress Press, 2002, 369-72, for a discussion of the genre and context of the Lukan version of the story from the perspective of a history of religions.

misunderstanding, as we shall presently see. But it is as the LXX translation of *kabod* that it is of real interest to him, since it describes perfectly the role which he wants to ascribe to Jesus, namely that of Revealer of the Father. The Prologue ends by reiterating the claims for Jesus, as Logos, already set out: 'No one has ever seen God. The only Son [some manuscripts have 'God'] who is in the bosom of the Father, he has made him known (Jn 1:18). This is clear allusion to the Hebrew Bible's attitude towards God's self-revelation, but also his desire to make himself known and present through the manifestation of the *Kabod Yahweh*.[10]

Throughout the first twelve chapters of the gospel the 'work' of Jesus is described through various revelatory 'signs' as the author describes them, the first of which, namely the wine miracle at Cana, is characterized as a revelation of his glory, so that his disciples believe in him (Jn 2:11; *cf* 11:4,40). Subsequently, Jesus engages in other demonstrations of his glory that are not so successful with audiences mainly characterized as 'the Jews' simply, leading to disputes with them. Often the debates centre on the double meaning of *doxa* just alluded to. Jesus insists that he does not seek glory from men, but the glory of the One who sent him (Jn 5:41; *cf* 8:50,54). A little later in the dialogue the difference of perspective emerges, as Jesus challenges his opponents: 'How can you believe, who receive glory from one another and do not seek the glory that comes from the only God?' (5:44). A similar pattern emerges in the seventh chapter. Again Jesus asserts his credentials to be from God by declaring: 'The one seeking the glory of the one who sent him, this one is true and there is no evil in him'. This contrasts with 'the one who speaks on his own authority and is seeking his own glory' (Jn 7:18). The Book of the Signs ends with a highly ironic declaration by the narrator: 'Many even of the authorities believed in him, but for fear of the Pharisees they did not confess it, lest they should be put out of the synagogue; for they loved the praise (*doxa*) of men rather than the glory (*doxa*) of God' (Jn 12:42-43).

---

10. C. H. Dodd, *The Interpretation of the Fourth Gospel*, Cambridge: CUP, 1965, 201-12; R.E. Brown, *The Gospel according to John*, I-XII, (Anchor Bible) New York: Doubleday, 1966, Appendix I, 503f.

The second part of this gospel has often been described as 'The Book of the Glory' since the author does not treat the trial and passion story in the same manner as the Synoptics. Perhaps it would be better to call it the Book of the Glorification since the verb rather than the noun predominates here. Jesus describes his hour as the glorification (*doxazein*), that is, his return to the Father. Thus his final prayer (chapter 17) is not a plea for assistance in his coming 'agony', but rather an appeal that he be restored to his rightful place with the Father and that those who accepted him as Revealer might be saved from the evil world, thereby sharing in his glory:

> Father the hour has come. Glorify thy Son that the Son may glorify thee, since thou hast given him power over all flesh, to give eternal life to all whom thou hast given him. And this is eternal life, that they may know thee the only true God and Jesus Christ whom thou hast sent. I glorified thee on earth, having accomplished the work which thou hast given me to do; and now, Father, glorify thou me in thy own presence with the glory which I had with thee before the world was made ... The glory which thou hast given me I have given to them, that they may be one even as we are one ... Father, I desire that they also whom thou hast given me may be with me where I am, to behold my glory which thou hast given me in thy love for me before the foundation of the world (Jn 17:1-5,22,24).

Clearly, *doxa* and *doxazein* are highly pregnant terms in the Johannine vocabulary. In terms of the gospel's main purpose, namely to present Jesus as the Revealer or Word of God, the noun suggests both visible manifestation and deeds of power. The verb on the other hand points to a process, not in the sense of Jesus acquiring glory through his deeds, but rather returning to the source of his glory as the final confirmation of the claims which his life's work made, namely that he was indeed 'the Saviour of the World' (Jn 4:42). Or as the Petrine confession in this gospel summarizes its message so well: 'Lord, to whom shall we go? You have the words of eternal life, and we have believed and have come to know that you are the Holy One of God' (Jn 6:68,f).

CONCLUSION: DOXOLOGIES AND POLITICS

It is against this background of the central theological significance of the theme of glory in both the Hebrew Scriptures and the New Testament that we can begin to realize the importance for early Christians of the doxology in its various forms. As mentioned at the outset, the spontaneity with which Paul can interject a word of joyful praise and acknowledgement of the divine goodness can be attributed to his personal conversion experience, and his sense of the transformation that is occurring in and through his ministry to the various churches as an 'apostle of Jesus Christ'.

The renowned literary critic and New Testament scholar, Amos Wilder, once attributed this aspect of early Christian expression to the sense of newness that was the hallmark of their experience and existence. As such, Wilder believes that from a purely literary point of view the Christian movement had to devise new forms and re-invigorate old ones in order to do full justice to the events taking place in their midst.[11] In a recent study Jerome H. Neyrey has taken a somewhat different line, drawing attention to the common rhetorical features of this particular genre of prayer of praise in the larger world of early Christianity. In particular he draws attention to the terminology that stresses uniqueness. He examines a number of the ancient rhetoricians and finds a broad agreement with regard to which aspects should be stressed. Aristotle's *Rhetoric* clearly sets the agenda:

> In epideictic one should also use many forms of amplification. For example if the subject of praise is the only (*monos*) one, or the first (*protos*) one of a few (*met'oligon*), or the one who most (*malista*) has done something; for all these things are honourable (*Rhet* 1,9.38).[12]

But Neyrey goes further than mere rhetorical usage and attempts to introduce social scientific models such as honour/shame, patron/client, exchange/reciprocity – all of which can be shown

---

11. A. Wilder, *Early Christian Rhetoric*, Cambridge, MA: Harvard University Press, 1964, 1-17.
12. J. Neyrey, *Give God the Glory. Ancient Prayer and Worship in Cultural Perspective*, Grand Rapids, MI, Eerdmans, 2007, 112-19.

to have been operative values in the ancient Mediterranean world. His purpose is to shed light on how pray-ers might have understood their own words and actions *vis-à-vis* their exchanges with and approaches to the deity in that world. While such social scientific models have indeed much to contribute to a general understanding of ancient religiosity, I am not altogether convinced that they can enrich our understanding of early Christian prayer practices. The Israelite tradition had its own particular understanding of the divine world that did indeed borrow aspects from its Ancient Near Eastern setting. At the same time it also had a sense of being different from the surrounding peoples, one that seemed to become more pronounced in the later period as political independence was eroded. Early Christianity is an offshoot from this particular root, one that saw itself in terms of being the fulfilment of Jewish futurist/messianic aspirations. The form and content of its public worship and prayers were much more reflective of this strand of Jewish piety, rather than the generalized picture of 'Mediterranean' practices that Neyrey's social scientific models proposes.[13]

To this end one could, it seems to me, more profitably examine early Christian doxologies in the context of what we now know of the Qumran Essene understanding of worship. Following the publication of the *Songs of the Sabbath Sacrifice*, Philip Alexander has shown how the *Yahad*, with its strict observance of the purity regulations, saw itself as participating in the angelic liturgy that was being celebrated in the heavenly temple.[14] Following a study by Jewish scholar, E. Chazon, Alexander proposes three stages of mystical union (*yihud*) presupposed by these writings. Firstly, there is the idea of harmony between different spheres of God's universe, the created world, humans, and the angelic choirs. Secondly, humans separate themselves from the material universe in their praise and consider themselves to be in unison with the angels, praying both with and like them, though expressing their unworthiness. Thirdly, the distinction between angelic and human is removed altogether so that they form a single chorus of praise:

13. *Ibid*, 31-62.
14. P. Alexander, *The Mystical Texts. Songs of the Sabbath Sacrifice* (Companion to the Dead Sea Scrolls), New York, Continuum (T & T Clark International), 2006, 52-59.

'You have purified man from offence so that he may sanctify himself to you ... to be united with the sons of your truth (*Elim*) and in the lot of your holy ones ... to knowledge of you, so that he can stand before your face' (1 Q Hod, XIX, 10-14).[15]

The Revelation of John shares this ideal of the earthly and the heavenly worlds combining in celebration of the Divine Glory. This work, written in a time of bitter persecution of believers, gives us an insight into the importance of the doxology for the Christians of Asia around 100 CE. They defiantly worshipped 'the One seated on the heavenly throne' – not the Roman emperor – and their hymns of praise were directed to that One alone. John, the seer, is transported in the spirit to the heavenly realm where he experiences a throne scene, reminiscent of that of Ezechiel. The One seated on the throne is receiving worship day and night from 'four living creatures': 'Holy, Holy, Holy is the Lord God the Almighty: He was, he is, and he is to come'. At the same time the twenty-four elders who are dressed in white with golden crowns on their heads utter their hymn of praise: 'Worthy art thou our Lord and God to receive glory and honour and power, for thou didst create all things and by thy will they existed and were created' (Rev 4:8,11).

As the scene continues to unfold, the role of the Lamb who was slain is revealed. He is the Lion of the tribe of Judah, the Root of David, who has conquered, and he alone is worthy to open the sealed scroll that the One seated on the throne held in his right hand. As the plot of the work unfolds in subsequent chapters the message of the scroll becomes clear. It is a message of hope for those who had persevered, and one of judgement on the wicked world of Rome and its imperial ambitions. But before the seer's heavenly vision is completed, he first hears the four living creatures and the twenty-four elders celebrate the Lamb's achievement:

Worthy art thou to take the scroll and open its seals, for thou wast slain and by thy blood didst ransom men for God from every tribe and tongue and people and nation, and hast made them a kingdom of priests to our God, and they shall reign on earth (Rev 5:9-10).

15. Alexander, *op. cit.*, 103,f.

The counter-cultural implications of this chant are quite clear, especially in a province where Emperor worship was rampant and the universal claims of Rome's achievements celebrated. The final stage of the seer's vision turns out to be auditory as well. He heard the voices of many angels, numbering myriads of myriads chanting 'Worthy is the Lamb that was slain to receive power, riches, wisdom, strength, honour, glory, and blessing' (Rev 5:12). But suddenly the earthly chorus joins in the chant also:

> And I heard every creature in heaven and on earth and under the earth, and in the sea and all therein, saying: 'To him who sits upon the throne and to the Lamb be blessing and honour and glory and might for ever and ever.' And the four living creatures said 'Amen' and the elders fell down and worshipped (Rev 5:13f).

In this sequence of doxologies 'the One who sits upon the throne' and the Lamb were celebrated separately. Now, however, in the final chant both are united in the hymn of praise that issues from the whole creation. One wonders how Pliny, who governed in the neighbouring province of Bithynia shortly after this work appeared, might have changed his report to the Emperor Trajan, had he had the opportunity to hear the Christian hymns to Christ as to a God, and understand their underlying message! Sadly in today's Christian assemblies the political aspect of our doxological responses to the story of the Lamb who has been slain have become muted. We need to recover something of their vigour, if the Christian message is to have an impact on our broken world.

CHAPTER TWELVE

The Lord's Prayer

LEONARD DOOHAN

THE NEW TESTAMENT contains two versions of the Lord's Prayer, one in Matthew (6:9-13) and the other in Luke (11:2-4). Matthew's version seems to be the basis for the prayer as found in the *Didache* (VIII:2). The two gospels were written around 75-85 and the *Didache* sometime later. Together they give us insight into both Jesus' prayer and the prayer of the early Christian community. The two gospel versions have many common elements, giving rise to discussion regarding a possible original format modified either by the evangelists or by the prior adaptations of their communities, especially for differing liturgical contexts. The prayer, preserved only in Greek, seems based on an original Aramaic version, Jesus' own language.

As indicated in the table [*on following page*], the structure and content of both gospel versions are the same, pointing to essential agreement seen in a common form that has been moulded according to different community needs. [Our table includes also the *Didache* text.] Luke's version contains five petitions and Matthew's seven (seven being the Jewish number for fulness and completion). There are some common components and an important parenthesis. Most have parallels in Jewish prayers of Jesus' time. When a person comes to pray he or she should first of all address God as Father then recognize three aspects of life with God:

1. Recognize that God's name be sanctified.
2. Recognize that God's kingdom must come.
3. Acknowledge that God's will be done (*only in Matthew*).

Following this come three requests on behalf of the Christian community, that have a present as well as an eschatological dimension.

MATTHEW 6:9-13	DIDACHÊ VIII:2-3	LUKE 11:2-4
Pray then like this:	Pray as the Lord enjoined in His Gospel, thus:	When you pray, say:
Our Father, who art in heaven,	Our Father, who are in heaven,	Father,
hallowed be thy name.	hallowed be thy name,	Hallowed be thy name.
Thy kingdom come,	Thy kingdom come,	Thy kingdom come.
thy will be done, on earth as it is in heaven.	Thy will be done, as in heaven, so also on earth;	
Give us this day our daily bread;	Give us this day our daily bread,	Give us each day our daily bread;
And forgive us our debts	And forgive us our debt	And forgive us our sins,
as we also have forgiven our debtors;	As we forgive our debtors,	For we ourselves forgive every one who is indebted to us;
And lead us not into temptation,	And lead us not into temptation,	And lead us not into temptation.
but deliver us from evil. (*or* the evil one).	But deliver us from the evil one,	
*For thine is the kingdom, the power and the glory, for ever.	For thine is the power and the glory for ever.	
*An addition found in some manuscripts.	Say this prayer three times every day.	

152

4. A request for daily bread (or for participation in the eternal banquet).

5. A request for forgiveness (or for final forgiveness). This is followed by a parenthesis in which the disciple promises to forgive others their failures.

6. A request for help to avoid temptation... (*and, in Matthew:*)

7. A request for delivery from evil's onslaught.

MATTHEW

Matthew introduces his version of the Lord's Prayer in the Sermon on the Mount, the first of five great homiletic exhortations that Jesus gives to outline the requirements for life in the Kingdom of Heaven. This sermon deals with the holiness of life needed by those who wish to participate in the Kingdom. Their dedication will bring them happiness (the eight beatitudes), their holiness must be of sign value to others (they must be salt to the earth), it must include a new approach to the inner spirit of ethical living (the six antitheses), and it requires the reformation of three great works of piety (almsgiving, prayer, and fasting). It is here, before going on to present further instructions for living in the Kingdom, that Matthew introduces his version of the Lord's Prayer, as part of Jesus' teaching on the transformation of piety. It is longer than Luke's version, divided into seven petitions, has a more Jewish flavour to it – Aramaic substratum, rhythm, and parallels[1] – and seems more of a liturgical elaboration than a private prayer. The first three petitions are in the passive voice and deal with the action of God in the world: sanctifying God's own name, spreading the Kingdom, and effecting his will. The remaining four petitions deal with God's care of the Church. The disciples pledge but one thing, namely to be reconciled among themselves.

In one of his books, Wilfrid Harrington tells the gospel story as if Jesus is narrating it rather than the evangelist. He puts this section very simply:

As for prayer: ask . . . seek . . . knock! —even though your Father knows your need before you ask him. Why ask then?

1. Wilfrid J.Harrington, *Record of Fulfillment*, Chicago, Priory Press, 1966, 71.

God does not need your prayer. But you need God; you need to acknowledge your dependence on him. And only in relation to God can you become fully human. You must acknowledge your dependence; you must seek and knock. The need is yours not his. Think of mother and child: a loving mother knows what is best for her child. The child may ask, may demand; but she will give only what is helpful. A firm 'no' is often the most loving answer. A loving Father will give, will open the way – but only when it is best. Never forget that 'no' is quite as much an answer as 'yes' – even to prayer![2]

LUKE

Luke places his version of the Lord's Prayer during the journey to Jerusalem, within his 'handbook' on discipleship where he summarizes Jesus' instruction on the challenges of the Christian way of life. During this journey Jesus gives two presentations on prayer (Lk 11:1-13; 18:1-8). The first of these is a small treatise in three parts: how to pray, the need for persistence in prayer, and confidence in prayer. The disciples have seen how important prayer is to Jesus and, seeing him at prayer (Lk 11:1), approach him and ask him to teach them. The result is the 'Our Father'. Both the context and the shorter version of Luke are probably more historically accurate; it would be unthinkable that an evangelist would deliberately omit a petition known to have come from Jesus. This disciples' prayer stresses the glory and Fatherhood of God, hope for the Messianic Kingdom and its benefits, as well as sorrow and forgiveness. Jesus tells the disciples that in prayer they too ought to call God 'Father', up to this point a title original and exclusive to his own relationship with God. They too may now share this special and intimate relationship. The disciple looking to God as Father addresses two petitions. The passive form suggests that the disciple should recognize that the Father sanctifies his own name and spreads his Kingdom. Jesus' words thus become both prayer and warning to the disciple that his or her contributions amount to nothing (Lk 17:10). The whole prayer, in the plural

---

2. Wilfrid J.Harrington, *The Jesus Story*, Collegeville MN, Liturgical Press, 1991, 68.

throughout, reminds us that prayer must always be communitarian and ecclesial. The disciple prays for three needs in the Church: a share in the bread of tomorrow's eschatological banquet, forgiveness of sins, and protection from the final trial of evil. The disciple's only action in the prayer is forgiveness.

Wilfrid Harrington gives this section thus, again as if Jesus is personally talking to us:

> At every opportunity, I withdrew for quiet prayer. My disciples came upon me in prayer and, deeply impressed, asked me to teach them to pray – as John had taught his disciples. I taught them to address God, simply and confidently, as Abba. They should pray that God will openly manifest his glory, bring about his Kingdom, so that all will be subject to him, and his Rule be finally acknowledged on earth, as it now is in heaven. Then they should pray for their daily needs. They should ask the loving Father to grant them his forgiveness – and the grace that they be willing to extend that forgiveness to others. And pray: 'Do not allow us to succumb to temptation'![3]

COMPONENTS OF THE LORD'S PRAYER[4]

Introduction (Mt 6:5-9; Lk 11:1-2)

In Matthew, as we said, the Prayer comes in the Sermon on the Mount, in the context of Jesus teaching his disciples how they ought to approach three key practices of piety: almsgiving, prayer, and fasting. Regarding their prayer Jesus tells them that they must avoid the conduct of hypocrites who pray for show, so that others will notice them, nor must they pile up useless words as if more is better than the depth of relationship. So, in Matthew, Jesus offers this prayer as a substitute for the wrong kind of prayer. He urges them to develop a simple prayer of union with God and he tells them, 'your Father sees you', 'your Father knows what you need'. 'Pray then like this', he concludes, and gives them the Our Father.

---

3. Wilfrid J. Harrington, *The Jesus Story*, 111.
4. See the step by step commentary in Wilfrid J. Harrington, *Come Lord Jesus: A Biblical Retreat*, Staten Island NY, Alba House, 1968, 112-19.

Luke's text often shows Jesus praying, and the disciples have seen this (Lk 3:21; 5:16; 6:12; 9:18; 22:32; 23:34, 46); besides, they have heard the Lord recommending prayer (Lk 11:5-13; 18:1-8, 11,13; 22:40). In the text we are dealing with, they once more see Jesus praying, they appreciate yet again how important it is to him, and so they ask, 'Lord teach us to pray, as John taught his disciples'. And so Jesus tells them that when they pray they should pray with the sentiments of the Our Father. A unique form of prayer was often characteristic of a particular religious group that wanted its own identity, and it is natural that the disciples want their form of prayer as John's disciples and disciples of other groups had theirs.

The Address (Mt 6:9b-c; Lk 11:2b)

Judaism frequently spoke of God as father or mother, including emphasis on the intimacy of this relationship (Deut 1:31; 8:5; 32:6; Isa 49:15; 63:8, 16; 64 8; Jer 3:4,19; Hos 11:1; Mal 1:6; 2:10). Later Judaism focused more on the distance, reverence, and holiness of God, and the intimacy of 'Father' receded somewhat. Matthew uses 'Father in heaven' twenty times, and this reflects the reverential approach of Jewish usage. Jesus refers to God as 'my father' (Mt 10:32-33; 12:50; 16:17) and tells the disciples that God is 'your father' (Mt 5:16,45,48) but only here (6:9) is the term 'Our Father', *pater hymon*, found in Matthew.

Luke's approach reflects a non-Jewish community. Although he too begins with the word 'Father' (*pater*), a form of address to God used by Jesus himself (Lk 10:21; 22:42), in Luke it seems to come closer to *Abba*, the way Jesus addresses the Father in Mark 14:36, and was later taken up by the early Christian community (Rom 8:15; Gal 4:6).[5] This more intimate sense of the term is original in early Christianity, a personal and individual address to God rather than the communal, even nationalistic form, that Matthew's use of *pater* seems to reflect. Luke's use of it makes prayer a matter of intimate experience and not only of theological conviction, and sets the scene for what is unique about belonging to Jesus' community of disciples.

5. See 'Abba', in Wilfrid J.Harrington, *The Prodigal Father: Approaching the God of Love*, Wilmington DE, Michael Glazier Inc., 4-5.

First prayer (Mt 6:9c; Lk 11:2c) – hallowed be thy name

The three hopes expressed by Matthew are all variations on this first one, that God's name be sanctified, God's kingdom come, and God's will be done. The passive is the typical language of prayer, while confirming that they who pray are simply recognizing God's awesome nature, presence, and power in our world. In Judaism, the 'name' refers to the reality of the nature of God (2 Sam 6:2; Jer 7:11; Am 9:12). This is not a prayer of request but a praise and blessing of the name of God similar to many such prayers found in Judaism. 'Jesus himself, when the hour of return to his Father was at hand, could pray: "Father, glorify your name", and the Father could answer: "I have glorified it and I will glorify it again" (Jn 12:28)'.[6]

The community in prayer recognizes that it is God, and none other, who sanctifies the divine name (Ezek 36:23), and the community blesses the self-manifestation of God. There is nothing in this or the next two prayers that the Christian community can achieve. Rather, their task is simply to appreciate the greatness of God. Holiness means 'set apart' and the community will be called to holiness – to see themselves as set apart to be God's chosen people (Mt 5:48). While it is God who achieves sanctification, men and women must recognize and worship the Lord.

Second prayer (Mt 6:10a; Luke 11:2d) – thy kingdom come

While this recognition of God – 'thy kingdom come' – is typical in Judaism, it is now found within the context of Jesus' own teaching on the Kingdom and on the role and obligations of the Christian community. As with other parts of the Our Father, this prayer also implies a hope for the final realization of God's reign at the end of time. Only the Father knows when this will happen (Mt 24:36); the disciples reverentially acknowledge that God achieves this when desired, and they simply give their faith and obedience.

In a variant of Luke's statement we read: 'May your Holy Spirit come upon us and cleanse us', clearly a Christian interpretation of the verse, possibly within a baptismal context. This baptismal

6. Wilfrid J. Harrington, *Come Lord Jesus*, 113.

interpretation, together with a Eucharistic interpretation of 'daily bread', seem like later attempts to link this prayer with the Christian sacraments.

Third prayer (Mt 6:10b-c) – thy will be done

This is present only in Matthew's version and fits in precisely with his theology of the will of God (Mt 7:21; 12:50; 18:14; 21:31). It is the way in which God's holiness and God's Kingdom are realized in practice. 'On earth as it is in heaven' can equally be applied to all three prayers – that the Father accomplish all this. In the Gethsemane episode Matthew presents Jesus as the model of perfect fulfilment of the will of God (Mt 26:39,42). The Christian community prays that God's will be done on earth, that is, in human society and in social interactions.

First petition (Mt 6:11; Lk 11:3) – daily bread

In the remaining petitions the verbs are active: the requests are made on behalf of the struggling Church community. The first two have the same parallel structure. They have taken on a double function of concrete practical need and a request concerning inclusion in the community of the end of time. 'Daily' can mean today's bread or tomorrow's. This is similar to the gift of manna, collected each day for sustenance and then before the Sabbath for the morrow (Ex 16:4-5). This can then lead into an appeal to participate in the grand banquet at the end of time – the bread of the final Tomorrow (see Lk 22:16,30).

While 'daily bread' or 'tomorrow's bread' refers in the first place to daily sustenance, and then to participation in the final banquet, it was natural, following Luke's own emphasis on the breaking of bread (Lk 24:35; Acts 2:46; 20:7,11), that later writers should give this passage a Eucharistic interpretation.

Second petition (Mt 6:12; Lk 11:4a) – forgive us … as we forgive

Matthew refers to debts, but Luke to sins. Matthew is probably correct in his use of 'debts' since that is picked up in the second part of the petition by both writers. This second part, almost a condition associated with the first, refers to the need of mutual forgiveness and reconciliation, a teaching frequently found in both evangelists (Mt 18:23-35); Lk 6:36; 17:3-4). While the Our Father has an eschatological focus throughout, it also evidences, as here, practical application to daily life (see also Mk 11:25; Mt 5:23-24).

Third petition (Mt 6:13a; Lk 11:4b) – lead us not into temptation

This request is to save the community from the final trial (see Rev 3:10). It hardly means protection from daily temptations but over time has been applied practically to such, and even Jesus who was the community's model in resisting temptation (Mt 4:1-11; Lk 4:1-13) urged his disciples in this regard (Mt 26:41). The addition in Matthew, 'but deliver us from evil' (6:13b), reflects a sentiment in the early Church, a desire to be protected from apostasy (*cf* 2 Thess 2:3-10). Some manuscripts of Matthew refer to deliverance from the Evil One – a theme found also in Mt 13:19,38.

Doxology (Mt 6:13c in some manuscripts) – for the kingdom ...

This is clearly a later, liturgical, addition that is exclusive to Matthew, though not in the oldest manuscripts. It is also found in the *Didachê*. It is most likely that when the Our Father was used in liturgy it would have had some suitable ending such as this.

PRAY THEN LIKE THIS

The Lord's Prayer offers a summary of some of the key teachings that Jesus gave throughout his ministry, teachings that together give us a picture of authentic discipleship.[7] Most elements have counterparts in Jewish piety, but the community can now understand each of them in light of Jesus' particular interpretation of each teaching. It seems that from the earliest times Christians used the Our Father as private prayer and as a communal and liturgical expression of prayer. The *Didachê* suggested that it be recited three times each day, and Hippolytus likewise urged daily use. More than Luke, Matthew gives the prayer a liturgical format; Cyril of Jerusalem first documented the use of the prayer in the liturgy, and John Chrysostom, Ambrose, and Augustine presume its use in the liturgy as part of the preparation for Communion. Nowadays, besides its individual use by Christians, it is part of

7. See Wilfrid J.Harrington, 'The Lord's Prayer', in *The Bible's Ways of Prayer* Wilmington DE, Michael Glazier, Inc., 1980, 125-27. See also chapter 9: 'Teach Us to Pray', 111-127.

the training of catechumens, is included in the Liturgy of the Hours, may be part of the Sacrament of Penance, and begins the Communion preparation.

So, the Our Father is what the disciples requested – a prayer that characterizes the community they formed, expressing their unique identity as disciples of Jesus. The list of components is obviously not intended to be exhaustive, but there is something about the prayer that is original in spirituality and becomes transformative for those who give themselves to its challenges. It cannot be overemphasized that within a few decades of Jesus' death the prayer he gave his community was already in at least two different formats, and the 'disconcerting'[8] differences bothered no one. The individual items were not important to the extent that the *method* of prayer was, the attitudes needed in one who seeks to pray within the context of Jesus' life and vision. The Our Father has four very special features that make the disciples of Jesus unique. I will deal with these now: (1) the call to foster an intimte relationship with God; (2) the need humbly to acknowledge a particular view of God in our world; (3) a complete abandonment to God's loving, providential care; and (4) the challenge to maintain awareness of two horizons of life.

1. The Our Father calls us to foster an intimate relationship with God

The use of the term 'Father' in the prayer implies profound trust and intimacy. A new relationship between believers and God is the unique characteristic of the Our Father – a quite provocative way of addressing God, in fact. Harrington draws a major conclusion: 'To proclaim that one believes in God is not enough. What matters and matters utterly is the kind of God in whom one believes'.[9] Led by his understanding of God as Father, he is extremely concerned to remove all false images of God: idolatry, a remote God, a law-giver, a God of wrath, a male God: 'The fact remains that false images of God abound – not least among believers'.[10] He frequently

---

8. Wilfrid J. Harrington, *Record of Fulfillment*, 106.

9. Wilfrid J. Harrington, *The Tears of God*, Collegeville MN, Liturgical Press, 1992, 11.

10. Wilfrid J. Harrington, *God Does Care: The Presence of God in Our World*, Christian Westminster MD, Classics, Inc., 1994, 52.

speaks instead about the God of love, the creator and parent, the forgiving God, the gracious God, the God-for-us, the grieving God, the suffering God, the crucified God, the foolishness of God, the tears of God, and he adds: 'God is God of compassion. Not a comfortable God – but so eminently comforting'.[11] Jesus insisted that recognition of God as 'father' was a requirement for entrance into the world, or reign, of God (Mt 18:3).

2. *The need to acknowledge humbly a particular view of God in our world*

The first three prayers of the Our Father (two in Luke) establish for the believer a clear picture of the world that is totally in the hands of God. 'The great throne (Rev 4:2) dominates Revelation, a constant reminder that God rules even in our chaotic world. Almighty God has a purpose and plan for this world. In dealing with the human world God will not proceed without cooperation from humankind'.[12]

While we acknowledge God as 'Father', the Prayer also reminds us of the awesomeness of God. God is involved in our world and even when we face great problems God is still always in control. The prayer reminds us that through all crises, God is and will be glorified, God's reign is and will be established, God's will is and must be done. 'God is Creator, sustainer of all that is, there is no situation in which God is not present, no place in which [God] may not be found'.[13] None of this depends on us; God achieves all. In facing our world we often feel helpless and cry to God to sort out our world that seems always to go in the wrong direction, asking God to bring about what we cannot. Jesus faces these day-to-day events and challenges us to pray no matter what happens. 'He has taught us to pray out of our day-to-day life. He has taught us to pray with confidence and with perseverance. He has taught us, simply, to pray as children of God to a God who is our Father'.[14]

---

11. Wilfrid J. Harrington, *The Tears of God*, 10.
12. Wilfrid J. Harrington, *Revelation: Proclaiming a Vision of Hope*, San Jose CA, Resource Publications, 1994, 110.
13. Wilfrid J. Harrington, *God Does Care*, 4.
14. Wilfrid J. Harrington, *The Bible's Ways of Prayer*, 111.

3. A complete abandonment to God's loving, providential care of all

So many people today feel empty and forgiven; they feel 'less' than they want to be, overwhelmed by the evil in the world. Without God we constantly go unnourished, cannot keep our heads above water, always fall short of our best, and drift to evil instead of living well. Jesus himself prayed, because prayer is a factor of our human condition. 'The prayer of Jesus, by example and not by contrived design, is meant to alert the disciple to his or her dependence on God. If the Son found a need and a joy in converse with the Father he could expect that the other children of God, his brothers and sisters, would, too, experience that want and that happiness'.[15] The introduction to the Our Father in Matthew reminds us, 'Your Father knows what you need before you ask him' (Mt 6:8; see also 6:25-33); so we can abandon ourselves to God's loving care and response to all our needs. The four prayers (three in Luke) focus on our conviction that the Father responds to our needs. However, each prayer is made with an awareness of community and of our mutual dependence before God. We cannot selfishly pray for our daily bread, or for forgiveness, or for the avoidance of temptation, or deliverance from evil, without thinking of others' needs too. 'God is God-for-us. The true God is God of love. God's love is not sentiment: it is active and efficacious love. Our response to God's love cannot be in word only; it must be in service. And the service God looks for is our service of one another'.[16] We all have a secondary but important role; thus, we too must provide nourishment for the hungry, forgiveness for those who offend us, avoid leading others into temptation, and deliver others from the threat of evil.

4. The challenge to maintain an awareness of two horizons of life

Believers have always understood the Our Father as presenting a double challenge – for the practical real needs of this world, and for the needs of the world to come; it focuses on here-and-now as well as on there-and-then. 'This prayer for the Christian community

15. Wilfrid J. Harrington, *The Bible's Ways of Prayer*, 95.
16. Wilfrid J. Harrington, *God Does Care*, 5.

suits the paradox of Christian life. We live in this world, we have a duty to the world. At the same time, as God's people, we are pilgrims on our way to our true homeland (see Heb 13:14).[17] Two horizons of life come together in the prayer. As we catch a glimpse of a realm of life beyond this one, we find new meaning in living in this one. In faith we know it is the world beyond that gives meaning to our world: 'It is taken for granted that a supernatural world stands above our earthly world. That heavenly world is the 'real' world. There is, indeed, a twofold dualism: the vertical, the world above and our world, and horizontal, our age and the Age to come. In short, the presumption is of an otherworldly reality which dictates the fate of our world.'[18] We pray for daily bread, forgiveness, freedom from temptation, and deliverance from the onslaught of evil, but what we really yearn for is to share in the eternal banquet, with the failures of this life forgiven, in a life no longer threatened by temptation, and protected from the powers of evil. These great hopes for the end of time are anticipated in partial realizations today.

CONCLUSION

Wilfrid Harrington provides an excellent conclusion for our reflections on the Our Father: 'Jesus taught a new way of praying. He himself talked to his Father as naturally, as intimately, and with the same sense of confidence and security as a child talks to its father. He urged his disciples to do the same. He withdrew prayer from the liturgical sphere of the sacral, where it had tended to be confined, and put it in the centre of everyday life.'[19] As disciples, we must do the same.

---

17. Wilfrid J. Harrington, *Come Lord Jesus*, 116.
18. Wilfrid J. Harrington, *Revelation: Proclaiming a Vision of Hope*, 8.
19. Wilfrid J. Harrington, *Christ and Life*, Chicago, Franciscan Herald Press, 1975, 33.

CHAPTER THIRTEEN

Communion in the Supper of the Lamb

SÉAMUS TUOHY, OP

I had the privilege of beginning my studies in Sacred Scripture under the guidance of Wilfrid J. Harrington, OP, at the Dominican Studium in Tallaght, Dublin, during the 1980s. That initial biblical formation in the Dominican Order consisted not only of academic courses in exegesis, but also of a pastoral and homiletic formation in the interpretation and application of the word of God, preached within the context of our religious community liturgies and the vibrant pastoral life of our growing suburban parishes. Fr Wilfrid's homilies were, and indeed still are today, an example of that clear and incisive exposition of 'the readings of the day' which becomes an authentic 'breaking of the word', seeking to nourish the lives of those gathered in that moment to 'form one body' in the Eucharist, the 'supper of the Lamb'.

'Blessed are those called to the supper of the Lamb.'

THE RITE OF COMMUNION, as presented in the Roman Missal, is a sober yet joyful ritual in which the faithful partake together of the Eucharistic Body and Blood of Christ, distributed and received within a context of prayer and reflection that is distinctly forward looking or eschatological in its thrust; 'that you may eat and drink at my table in my kingdom' (Lk 22:30).[1] There are many reasons

---

1. From the Greek *eschaton* (final, end), 'eschatology' refers to the study of end times or the final culmination. The Eucharistic liturgy is eschatological in nature in that it celebrates the 'we are not there yet' aspect of the Christian journey, and the challenge to live as fully as possible this time between Christ's ascension and second coming, *parousia*.

why this may not always correspond to what the celebrating faithful have in fact experienced at Mass over the past forty years, but perhaps a hopeful sign of recovering that eschatological dimension to our 'Communion' is offered in the new translation of the Missal, in which the scriptural reference to Revelation 19:9 is now rendered more explicitly than before, in the words used by the celebrant inviting the faithful to draw near to Christ in Communion.

Ecce Agnus Dei,
> Behold the Lamb of God,

ecce qui tollit peccata mundi.
> Behold him who takes away the sins of the world.

Beati qui ad cenam Agni vocati sunt.
> Blessed are those called to the supper of the Lamb.

In this invitation, citing firstly from John 1:29, the Eucharistic presence and activity of Christ are identified as the 'Lamb of God', at once evoking the ancient Passover liberation and its memorial sacrifice, and their fulfilment and completion in the Paschal Mystery of Christ. With the addition of the text from Revelation 19:9, this memorial and presence are joined also to the future, since partaking of Christ's life-giving Eucharistic food is already a share in and a promise of eternal life and blessing.

It is in the Eucharist as a celebration of the Paschal Mystery that the community of believers can find the past, present and future dimensions of time brought together. The Eucharist is not simply the remembrance of the Last Supper of Jesus with his disciples, nor is it simply the *re*-presentation of the sacrificial death of Jesus Christ; it is not only the participation in the real and active presence of the risen Christ in the Church and in the consecrated bread and wine, but it is also the *pre*-presentation of the *parousia*,[2] an anticipatory presence of the future coming of the kingdom of God, a foretaste of the fullness of joy promised by Christ and 'the pledge of future glory.'[3] This eschatological understanding of the Eucharist

2. This theme of the future coming or *adventus* of the Lord Jesus and the kingdom of God is recurrent in Mt 24; and in 1 Cor 15; 1-2 Thess; 2 Pet.

3. The concluding phrase of Aquinas' antiphon *O sacrum convivium*, for the Feast of *Corpus Domini*. See also St Thomas Aquinas, *STh* III, 73, art. 4... the *signum prognosticum*. In this sense every act of communion is also viaticum, or food for the journey towards eternal life.

involves more than an awareness or a glimpse of something good that is promised and will happen at the end of time, but it also concerns and influences how the daily life of the Christian community and its members is worked out and sustained here and now on their pilgrim way, confident, however, that the kingdom will come in its fullness, not as the result of purely human efforts, but essentially as the gracious gift of the Father.[4]

Within this dimension of the Eucharistic liturgy, and of the Communion Rite in particular, the NT themes of the eschatological 'banquet' and the 'supper of the Lamb' deserve some exploration and appreciation. Emerging from the Old Testament, both themes are transformed in the early Christian experience of the Eucharist as the sharing in our 'daily bread' as 'we await the blessed hope and the coming of our Saviour, Jesus Christ' (Titus 2:13).

THE ESCHATOLOGICAL BANQUET

'Blessed is the one who shall eat bread in the kingdom of God.'
(Lk 14:15)

Perhaps echoing a smug confidence in the promise of their guaranteed place at the eschatological banquet in the Messianic times,[5] this voice from among the other guests at a Sabbath meal in the home of one of the leading Pharisees tries to put down Jesus as he challenges them to abandon their preoccupation with social status and places of honour in table fellowship (Lk 14:7-14); 'all who exalt themselves will be humbled, and those who humble

---

4. See Second Vatican Council, *Sacrosantum Concilium*, 8; *Catcehism of the Catholic Church*, 1402-05; John Paul II, *Ecclesia de Eucharistia* (2003), 18-20. In his Post-Synodal Exhortation, *Sacramentum Caritatis* (2007),30-32. Pope Benedict XVI returned to this aspect again, convinced that a 'rediscovery of the eschatological dimension inherent in the Eucharist, celebrated and adored, will help sustain us on our journey and comfort us in the hope of glory (*cf.* Rom 5:2; Tit 2:13).' (32).

5. In the Old Testament, the kingdom of God understood as future salvation, was often described as an appropriation and celebration of God's blessing in the form of a feast or banquet, sometimes seen as a banquet that would extend throughout the messianic age; *e.g.* Exod 24:9-11; Isa 25:6-8; 55:1-2; 64:3; 65:13-14; Ezek 34:17-30; 39:17-20. See especially J. Priest, "A Note on the Messianic Banquet," in *The Messiah: Developments in Earliest Judaism and Christianity*: The First Princeton Symposium on Judaism and Christian Origins (ed. J. H. Charlesworth, et al.; Minneapolis: Fortress Press, 1992), 222-238.

themselves will be exalted' (v.11). As announced by Jesus, entry to that great future banquet will not be based on any claim to ethnic privilege – of having Abraham as their father – but must be based on a heartfelt response to the call to repentance, to humility and hospitality ... to discipleship. 'Then people will come from east and west, from north and south, and will eat in the kingdom of God. Indeed, some are last who will be first, and some are first who will be last' (Lk 13:29-30).[6]

In the course of his Gospel, Luke unfolds the meaning of the Eucharist for his readers through the teachings and parables and practice of Jesus, presented within the framework of the many meals he shared with his disciples and with larger crowds, his table fellowship with tax collectors and sinners, with dignified hosts and fellow guests of every kind. Through a series of ten meals,[7] different aspects of the Eucharist are revealed; the challenges of conversion and healing, of welcome and service, of giving and receiving, of nourishment and mission. For example, in the breaking of loaves of bread for five thousand people at Bethsaida (Lk 9:10-17), Jesus is presented as the host at whose table the crowds already dine in the kingdom of God. He is revealed as the Messiah (v.20), and for Luke the bread that is blessed, broken, and given by Jesus in the distribution entrusted to his disciples, is the bread of the kingdom. The abundance of broken bread left over is a sign that it will be sufficient to nourish the whole Church in its ongoing mission. It is

6. Luke set this particular saying in the context of Jesus' journey to Jerusalem, when some Jews who were following him ask whether many will be saved (Lk 13:22-30). He replies with the parable of the 'narrow door.' When the door is shut, there will be weeping outside, but many will come from all directions to enjoy the Messianic banquet with the patriarchs and prophets. Matthew used the parable of the 'narrow door' in his Sermon on the Mount (7:13-14) but kept this saying about the 'banquet' until the miracle story of the 'centurion's servant' (Mt 8:5-13) in which the Gentile centurion is presented as an example of one whose faith in Jesus and in his divine powers qualifies him to enter and partake in the banquet. In the Communion Rite, the text of the centurion's humble declaration of faith and trust (v.8) provides the fitting formula for the faithful in responding to the invitation to partake of the Eucharistic banquet; 'Lord, I am not worthy that you should enter under my roof, but only say the word and my soul shall be healed.'

7. Three meals during Jesus' ministry in Galilee (Lk 5:27-39; 7:36-50; 9:10-17); four during the great journey to Jerusalem (Lk 10:38-42; 11:37-54; 14:1-24; 19:1-10) and the meals associated with his passion, resurrection and ascension (Lk 27:7-38; 24:13-35; 24:36-53. See Eugene LaVerdiere, *Dining in the Kingdom of God: The Origins of the Eucharist in the Gospel of Luke* (Chicago: Liturgy Training Publications, 1994).

food enough for the journey. The kingdom that Jesus proclaims is already in preparation but will not be fully established until it extends to embrace all humanity. There is to be no turning away of the crowd (v.12) and the meal offered to the great gathering at Bethsaida already announces and symbolizes the banquet in the kingdom of God.

Later on, Luke presents Jesus' Last Supper (Lk 22:7-28) to his readers both as an account of the historical event and of an ongoing liturgical occasion. He reflects on the final events of the passion and resurrection of Jesus, but also on the living celebration of the presence of the risen Christ that continues to speak to the future, his fulfilment of the Jewish sacrificial meal of Passover and its transformation into the sacred sacrificial meal of the Lord's Supper, celebrated in memorial by Christians, 'proclaiming his death until he comes' (1 Cor 11:26).[8]

In Mark (14:22-25) and Matthew (26:26-29) the 'eschatological saying' of Jesus about not drinking again of 'the fruit of the vine' follows after the formulaic words of institution, where it evidently suggests that this Last Supper anticipates the Messianic banquet in the coming kingdom of God in which complete fellowship will be established.

Mark 14:22-25:

While they were eating, he took a loaf of bread, and after blessing it he broke it, gave it to them, and said, 'Take; this is my body'. Then he took a cup, and after giving thanks he gave it to them, and all of them drank from it. He said to them, This is my blood of the covenant, which is poured out for many. Truly I tell you, I will never again drink of the fruit of the vine until that day when I drink it new in the kingdom of God.'

Matthew 26:26-29:

While they were eating, Jesus took a loaf of bread, and after blessing it he broke it, gave it to his disciples, and said, 'Take, eat; this is my body'. Then he took a cup, and after giving thanks he gave it to them, saying, 'Drink from it, all of you; for

8. Luke's narrative is closely related to the liturgical tradition reproduced by Paul in 1 Cor 11.

this is my blood of the covenant, which is poured out for many for the forgiveness of sins. I tell you, from this time on, I will not drink of this fruit of the vine until that day when I drink it new with you in my Father's kingdom.

Luke, however, in his theological unfolding of the meaning of the Eucharist, relocates this saying *before* the words of institution. He reworks the saying, extending it into two parallel statements. Firstly, (vv.14-16) as an announcement by Jesus that this Passover he is about to eat with his apostles will be their final meal together, their Last Supper, before his passion. It is the historical dimension of the meal. Yet, he also outlines the future dimension, orienting their meal toward the time when his suffering would be completed, and he would again share in a Passover meal with them in the kingdom of God, inaugurated in the Church.

Luke 22:14-16:

When the hour came, he took his place at the table, and the apostles with him. He said to them, 'I have eagerly desired to eat this Passover with you before I suffer; for I tell you, I will not eat it until it is fulfilled in the kingdom of God'.

Luke 22:17-18:

Then he took a cup, and after giving thanks he said, 'Take this and divide it among yourselves; for I tell you that from now on I will not drink of the fruit of the vine until the kingdom of God comes.'

Secondly, the original saying about not drinking again the 'fruit of the vine' is taken up, and set more precisely in the historical context of the meal shared. If Jesus gives thanks for the sharing of this last cup with them, he will also ask them to share in the suffering that is imminent. The future dimension is also in view, to orient their sharing in the cup toward the wine that they will drink with him after the resurrection, signalling that the kingdom of God has been inaugurated. That fulfilment in the kingdom of God has begun with the Eucharistic meals celebrated joyfully in the apostolic Church as 'he opened their minds to understand the scriptures' (Lk 24:45), and as 'he was made known to them in the breaking of bread' (24:35). It will move towards its completion in the Church's continued trust in his presence and in her mission of faithful witness to the risen Lord, to his salvific message and the welcome for repentant sinners at the table of the Lord. It is not just an earthly meal – heaven too rejoices with the earthly community and the sinner sits at the banquet with Abraham, Isaac and Jacob in the presence of all the angels who rejoice in the salvation of the repentant believer.

THE BANQUET OF THE LAMB

'Blessed are those who are invited to the marriage supper of the Lamb' (Rev 19:9): In this case the voice, evidently that of one of the angels of the heavenly sanctuary, now echoes a joyful confidence in the victory of Christ, the slain Lamb, in whom alone lies the hope for his faithful followers of entering to share in the wedding banquet in the kingdom of God.[9]

5   And from the throne came a voice saying,
'Praise our God, all you his servants,
and all who fear him, small and great.'
6   Then I heard what seemed to be the voice
of a great multitude,
like the sound of many waters and like the sound of mighty thunder-peals, crying out,
'Hallelujah! For the Lord our God the Almighty reigns.
7   Let us rejoice and exult and give him the glory,
for the marriage of the Lamb has come,
and his bride has made herself ready;
8   to her it has been granted to be clothed
with fine linen, bright and pure' —
for the fine linen is the righteous deeds of the saints.
9   And the angel said to me,
'Write this: Blessed are those who are invited to the marriage supper of the Lamb.'
And he said to me, 'These are true words of God.' (Rev 19:5-9)

9. As an image for the messianic time of salvation (Isa 61:10; 62:5), the Banquet is here presented as a joyful celebratory feast for a marriage. It draws on the Old Testament theme of comparing Israel to a bride for her God (Hos 2; Isa 54:6; Ezek 16:7). The risen Lord is understood as a bridegroom who has united himself with the Church, his bride, who awaits his return (2 Cor 11:2; Eph 5:23,33).

Symbolized by the throne and the One seated upon it, the theological perspective of the Book of Revelation is dominated by the sovereign power of God over humanity and over all creation and the redemptive role of Christ the Lamb who shares the throne with him (Rev 4-5), yet in the inspired author's experience and that of the early Christian communities, there was also a realistic and painful awareness of malign forces opposing the completion of God's plan in the created world – the burden of evil accumulated in human refusal to accept the nature of being creature, the idolatry inherent in arrogant self-sufficiency and the diffusion of sinful greed, exploitation and oppression of fellow creatures.[10] Personified in the dragon and the beasts (Rev 12-13) these corrupt and seductive powers that continually rage, even against those who stand firm and cling faithfully to the ways of holiness, righteousness, and peace, seemed to threaten the foundations and the hopes of the early Church communities. With more than a message of comfort and encouragement, the author wrote prophetically for the Churches with a call to resistance and active engagement as faithful witnesses in a hostile world and to constant vigilance and humble repentance within the ranks of communities and individual hearts.[11]

That message and call are conveyed above all within the liturgical setting and format of the Book of Revelation, a heavenly liturgy in which the definitive intervention of God in the created order is celebrated and its completion anticipated. Victory has been won by God in Christ, the Lamb, through the power of the cross. The slain Lamb stands risen and victorious, and for the faithful also his cross is the promise of definitive and final victory.

Here the spatial dimension of transcendence, which is a feature of apocalypse, takes the shape of heavenly worship.

10. See Richard Bauckham, *The Theology of the Book of Revelation* (New Testament Theology; Cambridge: CUP, 1993); David E. Aune, *Revelation* (Word Biblical Commentary 52; 3 vols. Nashville: Nelson, 1997-98); Wilfrid J. Harrington, *Revelation* (Sacra Pagina 16; Collegeville: Michael Glazier – Liturgical Press, 1993, 2008), 23-33.

11. Richard B. Hays, *The Moral Vision of the New Testament: Community, Cross, New Creation,*A Contemporary Introduction to New Testament Ethics (Edinburgh: T & T Clark, 1997), 169-85, esp.173-75; Gerald W. Schlabach, "Breaking Bread: Peace and War," in *The Blackwell Companion to Christian Ethics* (ed. S. Hauerwas and S. Wells; Oxford: Blackwell, 2006), 360-74.

It is, indeed, a distinctive aspect of the eschatology of the work, in that eschatological realities are made present in heavenly worship. And because the Lamb appears in those scenes of heavenly worship, he thereby belongs in the world's present structure, for there is ongoing interaction between the heavenly and earthly. Worship unites heaven and earth ... Worship breaks down all boundaries. In worship all are equal. Worship establishes what is true, what is real. It is response to the admonition of the Lord: 'Seek first his kingdom and his righteousness...' (Mt 6:33).[12]

Revelation, of course, also uses the language and imagery of violence and destruction, even of the menacing wrath of God that is poured out against the forces of evil, and the Lamb itself is portrayed as a figure of overpowering strength and triumph, worthy to undertake the battle against the beast (Rev 19:11-21), yet there is no description of the battle here, for it is long over. That battle was won on the cross, not in an act of bloody aggression but in faithful witness and humble righteousness which reveal the face of God almighty. Despite ongoing conflict and tribulation and the need for consistent resistance, the concept of power is transformed in the author's theology of the cross; God's Messiah conquers not as a devouring lion, but as a slaughtered lamb (Rev 5).[13]

The symbol of the lamb also has a deeper meaning. In the ancient Near East, it was customary for kings to style themselves shepherds of their people. This was an image of their power, a cynical image: to them their subjects were like sheep, which the shepherd could dispose of as he wished. When the shepherd of all humanity, the living God, himself became a lamb, he stood on the side of the lambs, with those who are downtrodden and killed. This is how he reveals himself to be the true shepherd: 'I am the Good Shepherd

---

12. Wilfrid J. Harrington, *Revelation*, op cit, 30.

13. See M. Eugene Boring, *Revelation* (Interpretation; Louisville: John Knox, 1989), 112-19; Donald Guthrie, "The Lamb in the Structure of the book of Revelation", *Vox Evangelica* 12 (1981): 64-71; Sophie Laws, *In the Light of the Lamb: Imagery, Parody, and Theology in the Apocalypse of John* (Wilmington: Michael Glazier, 1988); Steve Moyise, "Does the Lion lie down with the Lamb?", in *Studies in the Book of Revelation* (ed. S. Moyise; Edinburgh: T.&T. Clark, 2001),181-94; Loren L. Johns, *The Lamb Christology of the Apocalypse of John: An Investigation into its Origin and Rhetorical Force* (WUNT 2.167; Tübingen: Mohr Siebeck, 2003).

... I lay down my life for the sheep', Jesus says of himself (Jn 10:14ff). It is not power, but love that redeems us! This is God's sign: he himself is love. How often we wish that God would show himself stronger, that he would strike decisively, defeating evil and creating a better world. All ideologies of power justify themselves in exactly this way, they justify the destruction of whatever would stand in the way of progress and the liberation of humanity. We suffer on account of God's patience. And yet, we need his patience. God, who became a lamb, tells us that the world is saved by the Crucified One, not by those who crucified him. The world is redeemed by the patience of God. It is destroyed by the impatience of man.[14]

Whether faced with life-and-death struggles, or challenged by real conflicts in daily life, the primary weapon for early Christian believers, as for believers in every age, is that of faithful witness (Rev 1:5; 11:3-13) and righteous deeds (Rev 19:8). With these, the followers of Christ, as individuals and as a Church, are united to him – and nourished on his gifts they are patiently prepared as his bride for 'the wedding supper of the Lamb.' The eschatological dimension of the Eucharist forms the faithful in the patience of God, in a patient waiting for the coming of the Lord.

Seeing Jesus coming toward him as 'the Lamb of God, who takes away the sin of the world' at the opening of the Fourth Gospel (Jn 1:29),[15] the Baptist already brings that heavenly vision down to earth, in the Word made flesh. This is the vision desired also by those who approach the altar at the Rite of Communion:

The action of beholding the lamb brings the beholder into such a realm of God-made beauty, innocence, and playfulness that, within one's spirit and in one's relation to God's Spirit, the killing weight of sin is no longer at centre stage. The burden, though present, is relegated to its place within the larger reality of God's creative and redemptive presence,

14. Homily of Pope Benedict XVI, Rome, 24 April 2005; Mass for the Inauguration of his Pontificate.

15. Jesper Tang Nielsen, "The Lamb of God: The Cognitive Structure of a Johannine Metaphor", in *Imagery in the Gospel of John: terms, forms, themes and theology of Johannine Figurative Language* (ed. Jörg Frey, et al.; WUNT 200; Tübingen: Mohr Siebeck, 2006), 217-58; Sandra M. Schneiders, "The Lamb of God and the Forgiveness of Sin(s) in the Fourth Gospel", Catholic Biblical Quarterly 73 (2011): 1-29.

within the unutterable world which is evoked by the wonder of the lamb.[16]

In the liturgical setting, at the opening of the book of Revelation, the author who reports his vision also sees 'him who loves us and freed* us from our sins by his blood, and made* us to be a kingdom, priests serving* his God and Father' (Rev 1:4-8). That same theme of Christ's coming which opens the vision dominates again the concluding chapter of the book. There the repetition of the Lord's promise, "Behold, I am coming soon!" (22:7,12,20) is matched by the invitation to 'Come!' – addressed to the Lord Jesus, but also to the Church, and to all who would seek salvation,

The Spirit and the Bride say, 'Come.'
And let everyone who hears say, 'Come.'
And let everyone who is thirsty come.
Let anyone who wishes take the water of life as a gift.
(Rev 22:17)[17]

The faithful wait to see him 'coming on the clouds' (Rev 1:7), but at the table of the Eucharist they are continually formed in the patience of God. They are prepared in 'Communion' to 'follow the Lamb wherever he goes' (Rev 14:4) in this world also, for it is a vision not of final escape but one that strives to respond actively even now and to welcome the coming of that kingdom. The Eucharist is not just a heavenly meal – earth too rejoices with the heavenly community and the sinner sits at the supper of the Lamb, in the presence of all the angels who rejoice over the salvation of the repentant believer.

16. See Thomas L. Brodie, *The Gospel according to John: A Literary and Theological Commentary* (Oxford: OUP, 1997), 152-57.
17. See Wilfrid J. Harrington, *Revelation, op cit*, 220-27.

Part Four

GOING FORTH

Pentecost

CHAPTER FOURTEEN

Ministry and Mission

HELEN DOOHAN

I FIRST MET Wilfrid Harrington when he was the Flannery
Professor at Gonzaga University in 1983-84. During that time
he gave a lecture on 'The Man Jesus in Mark's Gospel' that offered
profound insights for me as I was completing my doctoral studies.
Wilfrid spoke of Mark's testimony to the human Jesus who had
the fullness of God in him. It was an extraordinary statement for
me since I was struggling with the humanity and divinity of Christ
in the earliest NT writings. His statement was so deceivingly simple
yet theologically correct: Jesus 'is the one in whom God is wholly
present'. It opened the door for me to see Jesus truly as a model
for all Christians since we are called to live in such a way that the
fullness of God is reflected in and through us. Over the years
Wilfrid has developed and elaborated his ideas but his basic
convictions come through in each of his writings. He has made
Scripture accessible well beyond the academic community and
challenged people of faith all over the world to a more authentic
faith response. I count Wilfrid as a friend and gratefully
acknowledge that he opened the publishing world to me so many
years ago through Michael Glazier. To celebrate this milestone in
his life, I will examine the early writings of Paul, documents that
he knows far better than I do.

INTRODUCTION

While the whole of the New Testament offers insights into the
Church's understanding of mission and ministry, I would like to
focus on the earliest writings, the seven letters written by the apostle

Paul, namely, 1 Thessalonians, Galatians, 1 and 2 Corinthians, Romans, Philippians, and Philemon. In these letters we see the development and struggles of the early Church as it attempts to carve out an image distinct from its Jewish roots. We can identify Paul's exercise of ministerial leadership as he challenges communities to live the Gospel and grow in their commitment to the Lord Jesus. These letters also offer us a realistic glimpse into our beginnings as the Church because neither Paul nor the communities gloss over their conflicts or differences. I find it refreshing to see ground broken in terms of ministry according to gift, the equality of all in Christ, and the responsibility of believers for the growth of the Church, insights that still challenge us today in their implementation.

PAUL'S RELATIONSHIP TO JESUS – THE BASIS OF MINISTRY

Paul bases his ministry on his knowledge of the Risen Lord. Paul's knowledge of Christ is of Jesus as risen Lord, a direct result of his profound religious experience so well documented in Acts (9:3-20; 22:6-16; 26:12-18; *cf.* 13:47) and in his own writings (Gal 1:11-17; 1 Cor 9:1; 15:8-9; 2 Cor 4:6; Phil 1:12-14; 2:16; Rom 15:20-21). In his conversion, Paul's image of God changed so that he became keenly aware that Jesus 'is the manifestation and presence of God in our world'.[1] Hence, the focus of so many of Paul's theological insights and his own mission and ministry stem from his understanding of God's action in and through Christ.

Nonetheless, his Christology was so intimately connected with his ecclesiology that his proclamation of the Gospel and his ministry resulted in the formation of communities of faith. Paul asks, 'Who are you, Lord?' and the reply is 'I am Jesus, whom you are persecuting' (Acts 9:5). The uniquely Pauline description of the Church as the body of Christ, indicating the unity between believers and Jesus, results from this initial experience of the Lord. These insights influence Paul's ministry in the churches and form the convictions that emerge in his letters.

---

1 Wilfrid J.Harrington, *Mark: Realistic Theologian*, Dublin, Columba Press, 2002, second edition, 143.

THE FOCUS OF PAUL'S MINISTRY SHOWS APPRECIATION FOR JESUS' PRIORITIES

Although Paul most certainly knew of the earthly Jesus, the ministry of Jesus and Paul differed in some significant ways. That of Jesus was political, especially in his challenge to the Pharisees regarding the Law and its rituals as demonstrated in the controversy episodes in the earliest gospel (Mk 2:1-3:6). Jesus identified closely with the poor, outcasts and sinners, healing them and using their attitudes as examples in his teaching. He had a 'preferential option for the poor' and his ministry had broad appeal extending to all those in need.[2] Jesus was an itinerant preacher throughout the land of Palestine and his followers learned firsthand what was expected of them.

PAUL EMPHASIZES THE HOUSEHOLDS OF FAITH

Paul, on the other hand, engaged in political realities only indirectly as in his challenge to slavery in the Letter to Philemon. The sinful social structures were less important to him than Christian behaviour in the households of faith. Paul was provocative and controversial in his ministry but his focus was the churches he founded or intended to visit. In Galatians and Romans he addressed the place of the Law in Christian faith and focused on salvation in Christ in a way that challenged contemporary thought. Paul worked with leaders in the various communities and had numerous connections within the churches, as we see in the greetings and ending of his letters, as well as in Romans 16. The extent of Paul's ministry is the Gentile world and his travels, even by today's standards, leave one breathless, as he takes the message of Jesus 'to the ends of the earth'. He sees his ministry as expansive, even universal.

PAUL IS THE INTERPRETER OF JESUS' MISSION

However, similarities do exist between Jesus and Paul. Both proclaimed the good news effectively, both were prophetic voices in their word and work, and espoused values of forgiveness and

---

2 Wilfrid J. Harrington, *Mark: Realistic Theologian*, 27-28.

equality. They both respected women and attempted to overturn patriarchal influences through their ministry. A 'discipleship of equals' describes the emphasis of Jesus and of Paul. Both were guided by the Spirit and embraced suffering as part of their commitment. Although Paul never knew the earthly Jesus, his letters attest to the radical difference Christ makes, and he invites each community to focus on the implications of their faith in their daily choices. 'For my part, I became more and more convinced that no one has ever understood Jesus as well as Paul has. I have described him as the "exegete of Jesus" and so I firmly regard him'.[3]

PAUL'S MINISTRY OF LEADERSHIP IN THE CHURCHES

– Paul, pastoral leader, addresses the concrete needs of the community

In the letters of Paul, we discover a pastoral leader addressing the needs of various communities, with a variety of concerns, at different stages of their religious development. We can observe the dynamics of leadership at work in a period of crisis and change in the early Church. Christianity is spreading rapidly, away from its centre in Jerusalem and its roots in Judaism. Both Jews and Gentiles are responding to the message of Jesus proclaimed by disciples. It is essential to interpret the message for the various cultures and communities, addressing their interests and adapting to their language and social life. It is in the process of preaching that this interpretation and clarification of belief takes place, a fact attested to in Paul's correspondence. Eventually, this clarification of belief will lead to the radical separation of Jews and Christians, documented in Matthew's reference to 'their synagogues' (10:17). However, in his own ministry, Paul already takes the initial steps toward the final separation. Pluralism, diversity and sometimes division are the challenges for this formidable leader. He utilized a pattern of ministry that focused on handing on the tradition, while respecting local traditions, forming ecclesial communities rather than emphasizing conversion of individuals, inviting sharing and dialogue on all levels with the households of faith, challenging

3 Wilfrid J.Harrington, *Jesus and Paul, Signs of Contradiction*, Michael Glazier, Inc., Wilmington DE, 1991, 13.

inappropriate behaviour, and urging all to share in the responsibility for building up the Church. It is exciting, but also exceedingly difficult to interpret the Gospel authentically in these rapidly changing circumstances and for very different communities, but Paul does precisely this in his ministry.

– Paul's understanding of mission and ministry comes from his religious experience

Paul's understanding of his mission comes from his religious experience: 'But when he who had set me apart before I was born, and had called me through his grace, was pleased to reveal his Son to me, in order that I might preach him among the Gentiles …' (Gal 1:15-16). This passage echoes Jeremiah (1:4-5) and also identifies the extent of Paul's mission. He continues the mission of Jesus in his proclamation to the Gentiles, the formation of communities of faith, and, through letter writing, a creative substitute for his apostolic presence. But mission for Paul incorporates the vision afforded him that God now acts in and through Jesus on behalf of all people, a vision that gives him focus and energy in his proclamation of the Gospel.

– Paul's ministry finds its roots in theological convictions

Theological convictions are the basis of the apostle's work, but as an effective leader, he comprehends the unique situations of the communities and his letters respond to their needs, or (as in the case of the Corinthians), to their questions (1 Cor 7:1; 8:1) and concerns (1 Cor 12:1). Paul anticipates the potential problems facing a fledgling community in a Gentile environment in Thessalonica. But, he also urges that they assume responsibility for the direction of their church: 'test everything', 'build one another up', 'encourage one another' (1 Thess 5:11,19-22).

– Paul's ministry includes affirmation and challenge

Paul's usual approach to the various communities is to affirm their growth and offer seemingly exaggerated thanksgiving for their faith (1 Thess 1:2-10; Phil 1:3-11). His affirmations set the stage for his many challenges – a good principle for ministry today. When Paul faced serious opposition in Galatia, he registered his astonishment at their turning away from the gospel he preached (Gal 1:6) and omitted the usual thanksgiving, an omission duly noted by the community. Although controversial, Galatians remains a letter that establishes Paul's apostolic authority, presents a theological position for his interpretation of the gospel, and clearly shows the radical difference Christ makes in salvation history. Paul uses the hermeneutical key of discontinuity with Judaism in Galatians chapter 3, because they are too comfortable with Jewish traditions and rituals, while in chapter 4 of Romans he demonstrates continuity with Judaism for a community that must understand the scope of salvation history. If the Galatians adhere to Judaism, they compromise the essence of the gospel; if the Romans dismiss the influences of Judaism, they disregard the foundation of Jesus' message. This is a fine example of how different interpretations are necessary in order to address the specific needs of a community, an essential principle in today's very diverse universal Church.

– Paul's ministry also includes adaptation of the message to local community needs

The theological insights in Romans, the most profound of Paul's letters, address the needs of a community of Gentile Christians challenged by the return of Jewish Christians to Rome. To understand Paul's mission, we must appreciate how he adapts his proclamation to changing situations, grows in his understanding of the gospel, and applies key principles to daily life. While respecting traditions and handing them on, he reinterprets them also for specific community situations. His approach is also tempered by his own experiences. His travels and the exchanges with Christians on his journeys colour his ideas and expand his horizons. One of his imprisonments, which he believes may be his final detention, allows him to let go of his control of the message and affirm the Philippian community. What has happened to Paul 'has really served to advance the gospel' and the only thing to rejoice in is that Christ is proclaimed (Phil 1:12,18): 'Christ will be honoured in my body, whether by life or by death. For me to live is Christ, and to die is gain' (1:20-21).

– Paul's ministry is informed by his vision of the Church

Paul's ministry was also informed by his vision of the Church, an insight he received from his religious experience. He describes the community as the body of Christ and will draw out the implications of this relationship in his letters (1 Cor 12:12). A new set of criteria will replace the old. Paul's ministry of leadership includes engaging others in the mission of the Church. We read of the households of Stephanus, Chloe, and Crispus, co-workers like Prisca and Aquila, Timothy, Silvanus, Phoebe, Julia, Mary, Junia, and Andronicus. Paul relied on these Christians who were leaders in the local church and trusted them in their work in the various communities: 'Only let your manner of life be worthy of the Gospel of Christ, so that … you stand firm in one Spirit, with one mind striving side by side for the faith of the Gospel' (Phil 1:27).

– Paul's ministry includes partnership and collaboration

Collaboration and partnership in ministry resulted from Paul's insight into our equality in Christ, and this is clearly stated in his writings:

> For in Christ Jesus, you are all sons and daughters of God, through faith. For as many of you as were baptized into Christ have put on Christ. For there is neither Jew nor Greek, there is neither slave nor free, there is neither male nor female; for you are all one in Christ (Gal 3:26-28).

What a dynamic portrayal of a discipleship of equals we see in this earliest recorded witness to the development of the Church. The image of the body used to represent the Church is linked also with the new creation spoken of in Paul's letters. The new creation that is the Church relies on the power of the Spirit to transform the world; and the distinguishing mark of this new reality is love: 'Let all you do be done in love' (1 Cor 16:14). Paul also states: 'Complete my joy by being of the same mind, having the same love, being in full accord and of one mind' (Phil 2:2).

– Paul faces struggles in his ministry

While Paul's theological framework, experience of Christ, and vision of the Church are powerful motivators for him and set his direction, his ministry is not always effective. The letters to the Corinthians offer testimony to this fact. Misunderstandings occur and Paul resorts to defensiveness and 'boasting' to establish his credentials (2 Cor 11:21-31). But he also reveals his stature as a missionary when he reflects on the ministry of reconciliation: 'Therefore, if anyone is in Christ, he is a new creation; the old one has passed away, the new has come. All this is from God, who through Christ reconciled us to himself and gave us the ministry of reconciliation' (2 Cor 5:17f). His tone indicates his understanding of the issues at stake and he takes the higher path to peace and unity. I find it fascinating that the apostle spends so much time and energy with this community and sends them five letters (1 Cor 5:9; 2 Cor 2:3; 7:8,12), yet he fails to reach a mutual understanding, to clarify his positions, or to persuade them to follow his lead. In many instances, they seem to be ahead of their founder in their thinking as indicated by their questions and responses in 1 Corinthians.

– Paul's ministry is one of wise and prophetic leadership

Paul is a Church leader, exercising a prophetic ministry and collaborating with others in the spread of the gospel. His role differs from that of his co-workers and disciples but his vision inspires them, and us, to grow in our Christian commitment. The foundations of his ministry include his experience of the risen Lord, his theological understandings, and his vision of the Church. These experiences and reflections lead to the intense continuation of the mission of Jesus that we are privileged to witness in Paul's letters.

MINISTRY OF THE DISCIPLES

– Ministry is integral to the call to discipleship

Paul understands ministry as integral to the call to discipleship. We live out our faith in service to others just as Jesus did. 'For we are God's servants working together; you are God's field, God's building' (1 Cor 3:9). But following the Lord in faith has serious consequences, such as suffering, persecution, and hardship for himself and all believers. Prophetic witness invites the cross; if Jesus is our model, then death will precede resurrection.

– Ministry is the outreach of a charismatic community

The Corinthian correspondence offers wonderful examples of ministry in the early Church. We hear of gifts of wisdom, knowledge, healing, working of miracles, prophecy, discernment of sprits, speaking in tongues, and interpretation of tongues (1 Cor 12:8-12). There are apostles, prophets, and teachers who exert influence, heal, offer assistance, and lead the community (1 Cor 12:28-30). All these ministries are gifts of the Spirit and their proper use builds up the community, the Church. Participating in this endeavor is part of every Christian's commitment. To see the Spirit at work in the various communities is inspiring and uplifting for us today. To honor diversity, strive for unity, embrace equality, and affirm partnership is to emulate the essence of ministry in the early Church. It is to understand that we are the body of Christ, interdependent, and striving for unity of purpose.

– Ministry is a partnership of believers serving the community

The focus of the disciples' ministry is the local Church where Christians gather in the households of faith. In these gatherings women pray and prophesy (see 1 Cor 11:13). Heads of households include women like Chloe (1 Cor 1:11), deaconesses like Phoebe (Rom 16:1), coworkers like Prisca and Aquila (Rom 16:3), apostles such as Junia and Andronicus (Rom 16:7), all of whom are partners with Paul in the proclamation of the word. How seriously these people attempted to live out the principle of equality so succinctly is presented in the Corinthian correspondence: 'For by one Spirit we were all baptized into one body – Jews or Greeks, slaves or free – and all were made to drink of the one Spirit' (1 Cor 12:13; *cf.* Gal 3:28). Ministry is according to gift, not gender specific: 'To each is given the manifestation of the Spirit for the common good' (1 Cor 12:7). This way of understanding the work of the Spirit still challenges the 21st century Church, but we continue to be inspired by the approaches of the early disciples: 'Now the Lord is the Spirit, and where the Spirit of the Lord is, there is freedom' (2 Cor 3:17).

– Ministry is the acceptance of rejection and suffering

The portrayal of the early Church has a ring of truth when Paul describes the paradoxes of the Gospel message. Realism pervades as Paul speaks of power and weakness: 'My grace is sufficient for you, for my power is made perfect in weakness' (2 Cor 12:9). This power is the word of the cross, folly to those who are perishing, but to believers, it is the power of God (1 Cor 1:18). Although this makes little sense in Corinth, Paul views this understanding of weakness and power as life-giving for the community (2 Cor 13:4). Likewise, the paradox of shame and honour (1 Cor 4:10) is an inversion of the prevailing values in Corinth and has a prophetic ring to it. The reversal of wisdom and folly is a very unpopular position for Paul to take (*cf* 1 Cor 1:25). In fact, he uses 'wisdom' twenty-six times in the first four chapters of 1 Corinthians so that his meaning would not be misunderstood. Paradoxes present reality in a way that invites reflection on the mystery of life in Christ. They also suggest a realistic view of Christian values in a skeptical or unbelieving world.

– Ministry is a new way to interpret life

Transformation in Christ means looking at life in radically different ways than those who do not believe. Translating these values in terms of ministry means that the example of the cross of Christ is as valid as empowerment by the Spirit. Therefore, the disciples' ministry, while energized by the Spirit, is also informed by suffering, persecution, misunderstanding, conflict, and controversy. How essential is the theological framework of Paul's vision to enable us to persevere in the changing times in which we live. Ministry is a process, not a package. It calls for discernment of direction, not for quick answers. And if we are true to the apostle Paul, love is the guiding principle (1 Cor 13) and the key to our fidelity: 'Make love your aim' (1 Cor 14:1), for it is 'the love of Christ (that) urges us on' (2 Cor 5:14).

CHARACTERISTICS OF MINISTRY

Paul's letters, our earliest NT writings dating from 50-62 CE, vividly portray the growth of the early Church and present us with a living picture of Christian ministry some twenty years after Christ's death and resurrection. Several characteristics emerge that help us to understand important underlying principles and shape the parameters of our current conversation within the Church.

– Ministry is a response to real needs

The apostle Paul, and similar leaders in the local churches, take the pulse of the community, confront real issues, assess priorities, and address concerns. Each of Paul's authentic letters respond to, or anticipate, needs in the faith community. Situations are unique and differ greatly from the pastoral needs in Thessalonica, to misunderstanding in Corinth and conflict in Galatia. Ministry does not have a theoretical component, rather, a theological one with principles that can be interpreted and applied.

– Ministry is motivated by love

Several key values emerge in these writings that provide a context for ministry. Love is the overriding purpose and goal of Christian commitment: 'So faith, hope, love abide, these three; but the greatest of these is love' (1 Cor 13:13). The love of Christ and love of one another is the shining witness we offer to the world. On a par is our unity in Christ that results in embracing the equality of persons in the faith community and our new freedom in Christ.

– Ministry is interdependent and collaborative

With Paul's understanding of the community as the body of Christ, we must acknowledge the interdependence of all persons within the Church, and the diversity of gifts among these members (1 Cor 12:4-6). Each one is part of the whole, each ministry is essential to carrying on the mission of Christ; gift, not gender, results in the formation of a Spirit-guided Church. The partnerships that emerge in the letters between Paul, women, couples, and laity, and the assumption of responsibility for community growth by its members, challenge the Church then and now.

– Ministry guides growth in times of transition

Furthermore, ministry in a period of transition, leading to the Christians' separation from Judaism in the 80s of the 1st century

CE, necessitated a distancing from success or visible results. Effectiveness often happened on a deeper level, when disciples attempted to understand their roles in a changing world. Growth as a community, mutual responsibility and love, freedom and equality, celebrations of our life in Christ, and a vision that embraces partnership and paradoxes, are all part of the rich heritage we have from Paul's letters. I find many parallels between then and now that keep me engaged and hopeful about future possibilities.

CONCLUSION

Just like Paul's, our ministry can offer contemporary communities a vision of hope. Indeed, Paul's letters provide us with remarkable challenges as we minister in various capacities, and with limited resources, at this point in the history of the Church. Just as Paul respected tradition and developed it in light of new circumstances, so must we respect the tradition we have received from Scripture and from the Church so that a truly new creation will emerge again. The first-century disciples that come to life in Paul's letters offer examples and hope for dedicated Christians today in their vision of the Church. They saw great possibilities for the spread of the gospel in their world; new places fascinated them; people's ideas and interchange enlivened them. The breadth and depth of the missionary endeavors of Paul, and of early disciples, his contemporaries, affect our vision of Church and offer us hope in these early decades of a new millennium. However, we must also always remember Paul's cautionary tale: 'We have this treasure in earthen vessels, to show that the transcendent power belongs to God and not to us' (2 Cor 4:7).

CHAPTER FIFTEEN

The Presence of God

CÉLINE MANGAN, OP

R ECENT DECADES have revived a medieval notion of God being revealed in two books, the 'Book of Works' and the 'Book of Words': the presence of God comes to us not only through the Scriptures but also in creation.[1] This article in honour of Wilfrid Harrington will ponder something of how each of these two books can be opened in a new way in today's world. It is only since the Enlightenment that we have separated off the study of the world around us (science) and the study of God (theology). In his day, Thomas Aquinas could say:

> God cannot express himself fully in any one creature; and so he has produced many and diverse life forms, so that what one lacks in its expression of divine goodness may be compensated for by others: for goodness, which in God is single and undifferentiated, in creatures is refracted into a myriad hues of being.[2]

For Thomas, then, creatures can be said to be 'incarnations of the divine'.[3]

THE BOOK OF WORKS

As we learn more and more about the Book of God's Works, from the very great in the vast expanses of the universe to the very

1. See R.J. Berry, *God's Book of Works, the Nature and Theology of Nature*, London and New York, T&T Clark, 2003, 32-35. Earlier peoples saw no dichotomy between God's revelation in creation and in history: see R.A. Simkins, *Creator and Creation: Nature in the Worldview of Ancient Israel*, Peabody MS, Hendrickson Publishers, 1994.
2. *Summa Theologiae* Ia, q.47, a.1.
3. J. Feehan, *The Singing Heart of the World Creation, Evolution and Faith*, Dublin, Columba Press, 2009, 74. As a believing scientist, Feehan discusses the shortcomings of both science and theology on the question of belief in God.

small in the world of subatomic particles, our amazement and wonder can know no bounds. We are coming to know about new species every day: 'A single spoon of soil from your garden contains 10 trillion bacteria representing as many as 10,000 different species'.[4] Unfortunately in our time, largely due to human greed, many of these species are becoming extinct before we have even come to know them and to appreciate their capacity to reveal God's presence to us. The United Nations Organization designated 2010 as a Year of Biodiversity with the aim of raising human awareness and thus slowing down behaviour which brings about species extinction.[5]

There have been many ethical calls by Church leaders to safeguard the environment as the locus of God's presence. As early as 1990, John Paul II, in his encyclical for Peace Day that year, made the point that justice leading to peace for humans must also include justice for the earth:

In our day there is a growing awareness that world peace is not only threatened by the arms race, regional conflicts, and continued injustice among people and nations, but also by a lack of due respect for nature, by plundering of natural resources and by a progressive decline in the quality of life.[6]

But perhaps a call to ethical duty is not the first step; rather we should learn to be moved by the way in which nature manifests to us the presence of God. As an ecological poet, Robinson Jeffers, has put it:

This whole (the universe) is in all its parts so beautiful, and is felt by me to be so intensely in earnest, that I am compelled to love it.[7]

Theologians today can speak of 'panentheism' to express the realization that everything created is filled with the Divine.[8] This

4. Feehan, *The Singing Heart of the World*, 65.
5. See THE IRISH TIMES, 12 January 2010.
6. John Paul II, Peace Day Address, 1 January 1990, n.2.
7. Quoted in W. Fox, *Towards a Transpersonal Ecology*, Boston and London, Shamballa, 1990, 256. Fox goes on: '... this form of identification issues at least – perhaps even primarily? – in an orientation of steadfast (as opposed to fair-weather) friendliness'.
8. See A. B. Smith, *The God Shift*, Dublin, Liffey Press, 2004, 50.

is distinct from a 'pantheism' which implies that God and the world are one. The mystics had an instinctive realization of the presence of God in the world. As Nicholas of Cusa puts it: 'Divinity is in all things in such a way that all things are in Divinity'.[9] In a way the oldest example of this perception of the beauty of the world is Genesis 1 where we are told several times that God's perception of the world is that 'it was good' (Gen 1:4,10,18,21,25), indeed 'very good' (Gen 1:31).[10]

We are so used to thinking of ourselves as being over against nature that we must make conscious efforts to immerse ourselves in it and allow it to speak to us of God's presence. Ancient peoples did not think of themselves as outside nature.[11] Thomas Berry points out that it is only since the Black Death in Europe that humans began to see nature as a threat:

> Before the fourteenth century, Christian thought, for the most part, regarded the natural world as one of the basic areas where humanity came into contact with the divine. But when the plague (Black Death) came in 1347 ... there arose the difficulty of trying to explain in religious terms why a third of the whole civilization had perished.[12]

I recently spent some time near the Sheskinmore Wildlife Sanctuary in Kilclooney, County Donegal, an area which protects a rare and sensitive environment of sand dunes, tidal flats, and salt water bog. It is host to a wide variety of (now) rare plants, wild fowl and mammals. Being there, the only human being around, morning after morning, gave me a real sense of being one with the myriad forms of life around me, as each of us in our own way sang praise to the Creator.

Experiencing the beauty and the vulnerability at first hand should make us want to respond by preserving and enhancing the

9. Smith, *The God Shift*, 82.

10. See the chapter, 'Seeing with God: Israel's Poem of Creation', in E.F. Davis, *Scripture, Culture, and Agriculture: An Agrarian Reading of the Bible*, Cambridge, CUP, 2009, 42-65.

11. See Simkins, *Creator and Creation*.

12. T. Berry and T. Clarke, *Befriending the Earth: A Theology of Reconciliation between Humans and the Earth*, Mystic CT, Twenty Third Publications, 1991, 71.

biodiversity of life rather than destroying it. Liturgy is found not only in churches. Nature is indeed just as much the temple of God as the temple in Jerusalem ever was, as a nineteenth century spiritual writer on God's presence clearly saw: 'Nature is a temple. This universe of earth and sea and heaven – if it were not a temple, in virtue of God's perpetual indwelling – if it were not justified in recognising his presence in the phenomena of wind and rain, of production and growth, of order and change, of life and death – would dissolve and collapse in a moment. In that temple God is; well may earth itself keep silence before him'.[13]

THE BOOK OF WORDS

The United Nations Organization has invited people to look within their sacred traditions for resources that would imbue efforts to safeguard the environment with a 'vision of the sacred'.[14] While divine presence could be manifested in many ways in the Bible, such as in the revelation of the divine name to Moses at the burning bush (see Ex 3:1-15), or in the Exodus 'pillar of fire by night and cloud by day' (see Ex 14:19-20), the Temple in Jerusalem eventually came to be the place par excellence for experiencing the presence of God. In the setting up of that Temple, Solomon would pray: 'Regard your servant's prayer and his plea, O Lord my God ... that your eyes may be open night and day towards this house, the place of which you said, 'My name shall be there, that you may heed the prayer that your servant prays towards this place. Hear the plea of your servant and your people Israel when they pray towards this place' (1 Kings 8:28-29).

With the building of the Temple, the people felt that they had a tangible locale to contact the presence of God, especially in times of difficulty. For example, they believed that it was because of the Temple that Jerusalem was saved from devastation by the Assyrians when the besieging army melted away before its gates (cf 2 Kings 19). Ever afterwards they looked on the Temple as a kind of

---

13. C.J. Vaughan, *The Presence of God in His Temple*, London, Strahan & Co., 1872, 8.
14. See United Nations Environment Program, *Seoul Declaration On Environmental Ethics*, 1997.

insurance policy which would protect them no matter how they behaved, a fallacy that the prophet Jeremiah brought to their attention in no uncertain terms:

> Hear the word of the Lord, all you people of Judah, you that enter these gates to worship the Lord. Thus says the Lord of hosts, the God of Israel: Amend your ways and your doings and let me dwell with you in this place. Do not trust in these deceptive words: 'This is the temple of the Lord, the temple of the Lord, the temple of the Lord...' Here you are trusting in deceptive words to no avail. Will you steal, murder, commit adultery, swear falsely, make offerings to Baal ... and then come and stand before me in this house which is called by my name and say, 'We are safe!' – only to go on doing all these abominations? Has this house which is called by my name become a den of robbers in your sight? (Jer 7:1-4,8-11).

There is always the tendency in human life to settle God down, to feel that we have control over God when we have privileged means of access to God's presence.[15] In a way the story of the Bible is the story of how the people of Israel came to new insights into God and his presence and new ways of access to that presence. But once these ways become stale and empty they could become a block to the true understanding of God's presence. When this happened God had to 'break out'. As Carlos Mesters, puts it: 'All the supposedly sure lines of contact with God are cut ... God cannot be grabbed or lassoed'.[16] And Walter Bruggemann puts it like this: 'one can detect an uneasiness in Israel's worship traditions in the Old Testament concerning the divine presence. This uneasiness is rooted on the one hand in the affirmation of YHWH's freedom ... who will not be 'held' or domesticated by any cultic arrangement

15. See G. Neville, *City of our God: God's presence among his people*, London, SPCK, 1971, 20: 'The presence of God comes among men (sic) who live together in obedience to his own laws. They themselves are called to be the shrine of that presence. That shrine is always in danger of pollution by injustice and false religion; and if it becomes polluted, God is free to destroy it and build again, patiently build again, patiently gathering up the fragments that remain unspoilt, and creating a new people, a new shrine, a new locus of his presence'.
16. Carlos Mesters, *God, Where are You?* Dublin, Veritas, 1977, 95.

... On the other hand, the uneasiness about divine presence is rooted in raw, lived experience of absence'.[17]

The result in Israel's history was the destruction of Jerusalem and the Temple, the end of kingship, and exile to Babylon. This should have spelt the demise of their relationship to God altogether since, in the ancient world, a god could not be worshipped outside of a particular place. Instead of that, the exiles experienced a new and more profound understanding of God whose presence was not just to be experienced by them alone but by all peoples (see Isa 56:6-8). Return from exile saw the rebuilding of the Temple but by degrees there was the same tendency to feel that access to God's presence in the Temple gave one power over that presence.

THE TEMPLE IN THE FIRST CENTURY CE

The era into which Jesus was born was another era in which there was dissatisfaction with the way in which the presence of God in the Temple was being understood. The high-priestly families who oversaw Temple administration were considered to be venal land-grabbers in cahoots with the Romans who, under Pompey, had conquered the land of Israel in 63 BCE. Many groups voiced their opposition to how the Temple was being run, among them the members of the Qumran covenanters who had taken themselves off in protest to the desert around the Dead Sea to await a new in-break of God's presence in a renewed Temple. There are examples in their documents of impassioned addresses to the High Priest on how God's presence was being defiled in the Temple and in the land. For example in their commentary on the Book of Habakkuk, the 'Wicked Priest' is said to have 'committed abominable deeds and defiled the Temple of God'. He did this by 'robbing the poor of their possessions' (1QpHab 12:9), a comment explicitly related to the grabbing of land by the high-priestly families.[18]

Another counter-temple movement of the time was also concerned about the violation of the presence of God in the Temple

---

17. Walter Brueggemann, *Worship in Ancient Israel*, Nashville, Abingdon Press, 2005, 73.

18. G. Vermes, *The Complete Dead Sea Scrolls in English*, London, Penguin Books, 2004 new edition, 515.

linked to the violation of the land. The Roman conquest, and the incursion of Pompey into the Holy of Holies of the Temple which followed it, was such a violation: 'The lawless one laid waste our land, so that no one inhabited it; they massacred young and old and children at the same time ... As the enemy was a stranger and his heart alien to our God he acted arrogantly. So he did in Jerusalem all the things that gentiles do to their gods in their cities' (*Psalms of Solomon* 17:11-14).[19]

It is probable also that John the Baptist belonged to a group who challenged the status quo and believed that a new era and a new Temple was being ushered in (see Lk 3:7-9). Belief in the need for a renewed Temple because of the wickedness of those who administered the Jerusalem one was very much in the air of the Jewish world in the first century CE. For example in the visions of 1 Enoch the new heavenly Temple is extolled while veiled threats are directed at those administering the current Temple in Jerusalem. Seán Freyne shows how Jesus would have been influenced by such writings.[20]

JESUS THE NEW TEMPLE

The understanding of the presence of God in Jesus' time has to be considered, therefore, against the backdrop of the turmoil of the times. A recent book, *Jesus the Temple*, comes to grips with the intricacies of that background.[21] Nicholas Perrin argues that Jesus himself critiqued the Temple and the way it was being run (see Jn 2:13-22, and parallel passages in the other gospels) much as other groups of the time had done, precisely because it was no longer a fitting locus for God's presence with God's people. He looked forward, like them, to a new in-breaking of that presence in a renewed Temple, but unlike them he, and his followers after him, came to realize that he himself, by the overcoming of evil through healings and exorcisms and by his sharing of meals with the poor,

19. J.H. Charlesworth, editor, *The Old Testament Pseudepigrapha II*, London, Darton, Longman and Todd, 1985, 666; see G.W.E. Nickelsburg, *Jewish Literature Between the Bible and the Mishnah*, Fortress, Minneapolis MN, 1981, 203-12.

20. Seán Freyne, *Jesus A Jewish Galilean*, London and New York, Continuum, 2004, 157-63.

21. Nicholas Perrin, *Jesus the Temple*, Grand Rapids MI, Baker Academic, 2010.

was bringing about that new Temple.[22] The poor had lost their land through the incursion of the Romans and through the rapaciousness of the high-priestly families and others, and so in effect had become incapable of worshipping God as true Israelites: what was needed, Jesus surmised, was a new priesthood. Such a priesthood would need to demonstrate the core requirement of the priestly office, something the current priesthood singularly lacked: righteousness, a righteousness made concrete in caring for the poor.[23]

It was clear that the new Temple would only come about through suffering; just as the prophets of old suffered for speaking God's word so, too, the new action of God would entail suffering on the part of Jesus and his followers. The literature of the time speaks of the 'birth-pangs of the Messiah', taking up the idea expressed in Isaiah 66:7-14 about the labour that would give birth to God's new way of being present. As Perrin puts it in relation to the difference between Rome's way of operating and that of Jesus: 'Perhaps the most significant difference between Caesar and Jesus ... lies in their respective construals of power and suffering. For the Romans, the acquisition of power together with wealth and self-glory was a kind of norming norm ... For Jesus, on the other hand, true humanity emerged, at least in the present eschatological crisis, through the crucible of suffering'.[24] The Letter to the Hebrews gives great insight into how Jesus as the new high-priest of the renewed Temple inevitably had to undergo suffering: 'In the days of his flesh, Jesus offered up prayers and supplications, with loud cries and tears, to the one who was able to save him from death, and he was heard because of his reverence and submission. Although he was a Son, he learned obedience through what he suffered; and having been made perfect, he became the source of eternal salvation to all who

22. Perrin, *Jesus the Temple*, 149-82.

23. *op cit*, 146. Seán Freyne also highlights this: 'Pressure from the top inevitably led to an increase in the levels of poverty, and the slide from landowner to tenant farmer, to day labourers, to beggars, all characters we hear of in Jesus' parables, was inexorable. As always in such situations it is the poor who are most vulnerable, exposed to the effects of disease and dispossession' (*Jesus A Jewish Galilean*, 134).

24. Perrin, *op cit*, 187; see S. M. Schneiders, 'The Lamb of God and the Forgiveness of Sin(s) in the Fourth Gospel', Catholic Biblical Quarterly 73 (2011) 1-29.

obey him, having been designated by God a high priest according to the order of Melchizedek' (Heb 5:7-10).[25]

It is as if, in trying to turn humankind back to a realization of the presence of God, Jesus had to experience in his own flesh the pain of that turning. An old Irish poem describing the demands of love sums up for me the reason why anyone trying to do what Jesus did experiences suffering:

My love is no short year's sentence, it is a grief lodged under the skin, strength pushed beyond its bounds ... striving under water, outrunning the sky.[26]

'GOD DWELLS WITH US'

The early Christians explored all the places and rituals of their Jewish past to try to come to understand how the presence of God was revealed in the coming of Christ. John's Gospel in particular very subtly shows how 'in Jesus God dwells and achieves a communion of life with us that Israel had sought through cultic rituals'.[27] Further, John's emphasis on the mutual indwelling of God and the believer 'opens to all Christians the possibility of experiencing the divine presence'.[28] That presence is no longer to be confined to the Temple: 'Such is the radical nature of Divine dwelling in John's Gospel, wherein the Divine is not portrayed as a holy separateness, but rather as a "presence with" ... it is a "presence" that has its feet firmly planted on earthen-ground'.[29]

We have to ask ourselves where we are to experience that presence today. Perhaps, as in the time of Jeremiah and the time of Jesus, in the light of the scandals that have beset the Church, God

25. See Neville, *City of our God*, 62-66.

26. Quoted in J. Montague, editor, *The Faber Book of Irish Verse*, London and Boston, Faber and Faber, 1974, 68.

27. M.L. Coloe, *God Dwells with Us: Temple Symbolism in the Fourth Gospel* (A Michael Glazier Book) Collegeville MN, Liturgical Press, 2001, 219.

28. In a follow-up book, *Dwelling in the Household of God: Johannine Ecclesiology and Spirituality* (Collegeville MN, Liturgical Press, 2007), Coloe shows how the early Christians came to the realisation that their humanity was now the place where God's presence to the world was to be experienced.

29. C. More, 'Where Do You Dwell?' – 'Come and See!': Re-visioning Earth as Sacred Home, unpublished thesis, The Milltown Institute for Philosophy and Theology, Dublin, 2010, 69.

needs to 'break out' again from the traditional places where God has been experienced in the past. We could look at our liturgies with fresh eyes, in the light of our deeper understanding of the presence of God in the whole of creation. Our celebration of the Eucharist, for example, should be imbued with the realization that the Eucharist is 'the wonderful consecration of all earthly reality'.[30]

And so we come full circle from the Book of Words which tells the story of God's often fragile dwelling with God's people, back to the Book of Works where our experience of God's dwelling in the world is perhaps no less fragile. May we, then, learn to preserve our environments and habitats and renew our understanding of Scripture and Liturgy, as through his many writings Wilfrid Harrington has so admirably taught us to do, so that God's presence among us may be more deeply understood in our time.

30. B. Häring, *The Eucharist and our Everyday Life*, Middlegreen, Slough, St Paul Publications, 1978, 52.

Bibliography of Wilfrid J Harrington, OP

1963   *Explaining the Gospels*
       (Mahwah, New Jersey [NJ]: Paulist Press)

1964   *A Key to the Parables* (NJ: Paulist Press)
       [*He Spoke in Parables* (Dublin: Helicon)]

1965   *Record of Revelation: The Bible* (Chicago: Priory Press)
       Record of the Promise: The Old Testament
       (Chicago: Priory Press)
       Leabhar Dhainéil (with P. O Fiannachta)
       (Aonach: Cló Uí Mheara)

1966   *Record of the Fulfillment: The New Testament*
       (Chicago: Priory Press)
       Zeugnis der Offenbarung (Stuttgart: Katholisches Bibelwerk)

1967   *Il Parlait en Paraboles* (Paris: Cerf)
       The Gospel According to St Luke: A Commentary
       (New York/London: Newman/Chapman)
       Vatican II on Revelation (with Liam Walsh) (Dublin: Scepter)
       Iniciacion a la Biblia I (Santander: Sal Terrae)
       Hij Sprak in Parabels (Bilthoven: H. Nelissen)

1968   *Iniciacion a la Biblia* II (Santander: Sal Terrae)
       Come Lord Jesus: A Biblical Retreat (NJ: Alba)
       The Promise to Love: A Biblical View of Marriage (NJ: Alba)
       The Apocalypse of St John: A Commentary (London: Chapman)

1969   [*Understanding the Apocalypse* (NY: Corpus)]

1971   *Nouvelle Introduction à la Bible* (Paris: Seuil)

1973   *The Path of Biblical Theology* (Dublin: Gill and Macmillan)
1974   *Key to the Bible. 3 Volumes* (Canfield, Ohio: Alba)
       Parables Told by Jesus (NY: Alba)

1975   *Nuova Introduzione alla Bibbia* (Bologna: Dehoniane)
       Christ and Life (Dublin/Chicago: Gill & Macmillan/
       Franciscan Herald)

[*Key to the Bible*. 3 Volumes (NY: Doubleday)]
The Rosary: A Gospel Prayer (Canfield, Ohio: Alba)
[Japanese edition some years later]
Uvod u Novi Zavjet (Zagreb: Krscanska sadasnjost)
[Croatian version of *Record of the Fulfillment*]

1976   *In the Beginning God* (Manchester: Koinonia)

1977   *Spirit of the Living God* (Wilmington DE: M.Glazier)
Teologia Biblijna (Warszawa: Instytut Wydawniczy PAX)
[Polish version of *The Path of Biblical Theology*]
Uvod u Bibliju (Zagreb: Krscasnska sadasdnjost)
Uvod u Stari (Zagreb: Krscasnska sadasdnjost)
[Croatian versions of *Record of Revelation*
and *Record of the Promise*]

1978   *The New Guide to Reading and Studying the Bible*
(Wilmington DE: M. Glazier)

1979   *Mark*. New Testament Message 4 (Wilmington/Dublin:
M.Glazier/Veritas)
[Co-editor of *New Testament Message* commentary series]
Witness to the Spirit (ed.) (Dublin: Irish Biblical Association)

1980   *The Bible's Ways of Prayer* (Wilmington DE: M. Glazier)
The Saving Word. Year A [Co-author]
(Wilmington DE: M. Glazier)

1981   *The Saving Word*. Year B [Co-author]
(Wilmington DE: M. Glazier)
Klucz do Biblii (Warszawa: Instytut Wydawniczy PAX)
[Polish version of *Key to the Bible*]

1982   *The Prodigal Father* (Wilmington DE: M. Glazier)
The Saving Word. Year C [Co-author]
(Wilmington DE: M. Glazier)

1984   *The New Guide to Reading and Studying the Bible*:
New, enlarged Edition (Wilmington DE: M.Glazier)

1986   *Jesus and Paul. Signs of Contradiction*
(Wilmington DE: M.Glazier)

1987   *Chrystus i zycie* (Warszawa: Instytut Wydawniczy PAX)
        [Polish version of *Christ and Life*]

1988   *The Drama of Christ's Coming* (Wilmington DE: M. Glazier)
        Heroes and Heroines of the Way (Dublin: Gill and Macmillan)

1989   [*A Cloud of Witnesses* (Wilmington DE: M. Glazier)]

1991   *The Jesus Story* (Collegeville/Dublin: Liturgical Press/
        Columba Press).
        Az Iras Hosei es Hosnoi (Budapest: Vizonto Konyvek)
        [Hungarian version of *Heroes and Heroines of the Way*]

1992   *The Tears of God* (Collegeville MN: Liturgical Press)

1993   *Revelation..* Sacra Pagina 16
        (Collegeville MN: Liturgical Press)

1994   *God Does Care* (Westminster MD
        Dublin: Christian Classics/Columba Press)
        Revelation: Proclaiming a Vision of Hope
        (San Jose CA: Resource Publications)

1995   *The Gracious Word*. Year A (Dublin: Dominican Publications)

1996   *The Gracious Word*. Year B (Dublin: Dominican Publications)
        Mark: Realistic Theologian (Dublin: Columba Press)

1997   *The Gracious Word*. Year C (Dublin: Dominican Publications)
        Luke: Gracious Theologian (Dublin: Columba Press)

1998   *Hold On To Hope* (Dublin: Dominican Publications)
        Matthew: Sage Theologian (Dublin: Columba Press)

1999   *John: Spiritual Theologian* (Dublin: Columba Press)

2002   *Seeking Spiritual Growth Through the Bible*
        (New York: Paulist Press)

2003   *The Mysteries of Light. The New Rosary as Gospel Prayer*
        (Dublin: Dominican Publications)

2005   *Rozwoj duchowy inspiracje biblijne*
        (Kraków: Wydawnictwo WAM)
        [Polish version of *Seeking Spiritual Growth Through the Bible*]

2006   *From the Presence of the Lord. A God too Gracious*
        (Dublin: Columba Press)

2008   *What Was Mark At? The Gospel of Mark: A Commentary*
        (Dublin: Columba Press)
        Chave para a Biblia (Sao Paulo: Paulus)
        [Portuguese version of *Key to the Bible*]

2010   *Jesus Our Brother. The Humanity of the Lord*
        (New York: Paulist Press)

2012   *The Loving God* (Dublin: Columba Press)

Contributions to Collaborative Works:

A New Catholic Commentary on Holy Scripture
R. Fuller, L. Johnston, C. Kearns, eds, Nelson, London, 1969: 'Luke',
986-1021, and 'The Critical Study of the NT', 802-809.

An Biobla Naofa: An Tiomna Nua
P. O Fiannachta, eag., An Sagart, Maigh Nuad, 1981: *Brollaigh* –
Introductions: *Na Soiscéil* – The Gospels (pp 3-13); *Gníomhartha na
nAspal* – The Acts of the Apostles (115-117); *Litreacha Phóil* – Paul's
Letters (146-161); *Na Litreacha Caitliceachta* – The Catholic Letters
(230-234); *Apacailipsis Eoin* – The Apocalypse of John (248-249).

The New Dictionary of Theology
J. Komonchak, M. Collins, D. Lane, eds, Wilmington DE, M. Glazier,
1987: 'Abba', 12; 'The New Testament', 86-102; 'Parable', 739-42;
'Senses of Scripture', 945-47.

New Testament Message. A Biblical-Theological Commentary, 22 Volumes
Editor, with Donald Senior CP, Wilmington DE, M. Glazier, 1979-
1981.

Articles by Wilfrid Harrington have appeared in:

*Biblical Theology Bulletin; Doctrine and Life; The Furrow; Irish
Theological Quarterly; Priests and People; Proceedings of the Irish Biblical
Association; Religious Life Review; Scripture in Church; Spirituality.*

Contributors

Vivian Boland OP

A Dominican since 1971, Vivian studied in Tallaght, Edinburgh and Rome. He has lectured in moral theology and in the thought of Aquinas at Milltown and Tallaght, where he was regent of studies 1992-1996. More recently has taught at Blackfriars, Oxford and St Mary's University College, Twickenham. He was master of students of the English province and was director of the Aquinas Institute at Blackfriars. His major publications include *Ideas in God* (Brill, 1996) and *St Thomas Aquinas* (Continuum Library of Educational Thought, 2007), and he edited *Don't Put Out the Burning Bush*: *Worship and Preaching in a Complex World* (Adelaide, 2008) and *Watchmen Raise Their Voices: A Tallaght Book of Theology* (Dominican Publications, 2006). He is currently an assistant to the Master of the Dominicans based at Santa Sabina, Rome.

Thomas L. Brodie OP

Moderator of the Dominican Biblical Institute, Limerick, Thomas Brodie has taught scripture mainly in Trinidad, the USA, and South Africa. Since 1972 his life has been dominated by the increasing evidence that scripture study is moving to a new phase, essentially away from emphasis on specific historical events and toward appreciating scripture as history-like life-related literature – inspired artistic writing, including the systematic rewriting and transformation of older texts, particularly older scriptures. His books include commentaries on John (1993) and Genesis (2001), and an outline of the development of the New Testament (*The Birthing of the New Testament*, 2004).

Margaret Daly-Denton

The early career of Margaret Daly-Denton was as an organist and composer with an academic and practical involvement in liturgy. More recently, she moved into biblical studies, her doctoral research being published in 2000 as *David in the Fourth Gospel*. A second book, *Psalm-Shaped Prayerfulness: A Guide to the Christian Reception of the Psalms* appeared in 2010. Her current project is the volume on the Fourth Gospel for the forthcoming Earth Bible Commentary. She has taught at various institutions in Ireland including Trinity College Dublin, the Milltown Institute, The Church of Ireland Theological Institute, All Hallows College (DCU), and the Priory Institute.

Helen Doohan

Professor Emerita at Gonzaga University, Helen Doohan had been a Professor of Religious Studies and the Arnold Distinguished Professor of Humanities at Gonzaga. She is author of five books, focusing especially on the writings of St Paul, including *Paul's Vision of Church* (1989), *The Corinthian Correspondence* (1996), and *Prayer in the New Testament* (1991). She has given conferences and workshops all over the world. Now retired, she splits her time between the United States and Italy.

Leonard Doohan

Professor Emeritus at Gonzaga University, Leonard Doohan had been a Professor of Religious Studies there for 27 years and Dean of the Graduate School for 13 years. He has written eighteen books and 160 articles and has given over 300 workshops throughout the USA, Canada, Europe, Australia, New Zealand, and the Far East. His recent books include *Spiritual Leadership: The Quest for Integrity* (2007), *Enjoying Retirement: Living Life to the Fullest* (2010) and *Courageous Hope: The Call of Leadership* (2001).

Seán Freyne

Seán Freyne is Professor of Theology (Emeritus) at Trinity College Dublin. He has lectured at various institutions in the USA, Germany and Australia as well as at the Pontifical University of Maynooth. He is a past president of the Society for New Testament Studies and a member of the Royal Irish Academy. His published research work is in the fields of Early Judaism and Early Christianity in their Greco-Roman setting, with a special focus on Hellenistic and

Roman Galilee. He has published many articles and several books, his latest being *Jesus a Jewish Galilean: A New Reading of the Jesus Story* (2005).

Michael Glazier

Michael Glazier and his wife Joan, natives of Tralee, County Kerry, emigrated to the USA in 1956. Michael founded Scholarly Resources to publish Parliamentary Papers of the 18th century. His later publishing house, Michael Glazier Inc., has made a considerable impact, not least with the Commentary Series *New Testament Message* (22 vols) and *Old Testament Message* (23 vols). He also published the first complete English translation of the Aramaic Targums, and the first Catholic desk dictionary, *The New Dictionary of Theology* (1987). Michael has launched many young writers including several of the contributors to this volume and has been honoured by the Catholic Biblical Association of America and the Catholic Library Association.

Daniel J. Harrington SJ

Professor of New Testament at Boston College School of Theology and Ministry, Daniel J Harrington is also editor of *New Testament Abstracts*. He is a past president of the Catholic Biblical Association of America and the author of over fifty books. His scholarly interests include early Judaism, the Dead Sea Scrolls, the Gospels, and hermeneutics.

Thomas McCarthy OP

Currently editor of *Religious Life Review*, Thomas McCarthy was a pupil of Wilfrid Harrington in the 1970s, and, after ordination, studied early Christian history at the Roman Patristic Institute, *Augustinianum*, before going on to teach patristic and dogmatic theology in Tallaght. After that, he served as Secretary General of the Order of Preachers, assisting the Master of the Order and his Council in Rome, and has been working as editor and writer at Dominican Publications since 2003. Thomas still teaches theology, and for over twenty years has been an international television commentator on major Papal ceremonies.

Céline Mangan OP

It was at University College, Dublin, and at the *École Biblique*, Jerusalem that Céline Mangan studied Scripture, and she received the LSS from the Pontifical Biblical Commission, Rome. She has taught in various colleges and is currently Associate Professor of the Milltown Institute, Dublin. Specialising in Targum studies, she translated the Book of Job for the series, *The Bible in Aramaic*. Céline has also contributed to many journals especially to *Scripture in Church* and has wide experience in giving talks, workshops and courses to a variety of groups.

Francis J. Moloney SDB

Born and educated in Australia, Francis J Moloney joined the Salesians of Don Bosco in 1960, and has been Provincial Superior of the Salesians in Australia and the Pacific. After further academic and religious formation in Australia, he studied in Rome (STL, LSS) and Oxford (D Phil). He has a long teaching experience in Australia, Europe, Israel and the USA. He is the author of many books and articles, both scholarly and popular, on various aspects of the New Testament, and several studies in the area of Religious Life and Christian Spirituality.

Jerome Murphy-O'Connor OP

Jerome Murphy-O'Connor is Professor of New Testament in the *École Biblique*, Jerusalem, where he has taught since 1967. His research has focused particularly on the Pauline letters, on which he has published *Paul. A Critical Life* (1996) and *Paul. His Story* (2004). He has also written extensively on the historical Jesus. The two interests were drawn together in *Jesus and Paul. Parallel Lives* (2007). Fifty years residence in Jerusalem has made him an expert on its history and archaeology. A collection of his articles will appear as *Keys to Jerusalem* in 2012.

Mark A. O'Brien OP

A member of the Australia and New Zealand province of the Dominican Order, Mark and was ordained in Tallaght in 1973, where he had studied. He completed post-graduate biblical studies at the Pontifical Biblical Institute, Rome and the Melbourne College of Divinity. He is the author of *The Deuteronomistic History Hypothesis: A Reassessment* (1989) and has co-authored several books on the Old Testament with Antony F. Campbell SJ. He currently lectures in the Melbourne College of Divinity. He has also lectured in the Sydney College of Divinity, at Blackfriars, Oxford, and in Karachi, Pakistan.

Thomas O'Loughlin

Professor of Historical Theology in the University of Nottingham, Thomas O'Loughlin was for many years Wilfrid's colleague in the Milltown Institute for Philosophy and Theology, and in the *studium* of the Irish Dominicans in Tallaght. His research focuses on the reception of the Scriptures as part of the theological endeavour; in recent years this has led to a book on the *Didachê* at one end of the spectrum, and, most recently, a book on the hermeneutics of the lectionary at the other. He is editor of *Studia Traditionis Theologiae*.

Donald Senior CP

President of Catholic Theological Union in Chicago, the largest Roman Catholic graduate school of ministry in the USA, Donald Senior is also Professor of New Testament there. He is a frequent lecturer, serves on numerous boards and commissions, and is widely published. He is a past president of the Catholic Biblical Association of America and of the Association of Theological Schools of the United States and Canada. In 2001, John Paul II appointed him a member of the Pontifical Biblical Commission and he was re-appointed in 2006 by Pope Benedict XVI.

Séamus Tuohy OP

A native of County Kerry, Séamus was ordained priest in 1986. He studied at the *studium* of the Province of Ireland, in Tallaght, at University College, Dublin, at the Pontifical Biblical Institute, Rome, and at the Pontifical University of St Thomas (*Angelicum*), Rome. He has also been involved with pastoral, administrative, and teaching work in Trinidad and Tobago, Rome, and Ireland. He teaches Sacred Scripture in Dublin.

Liam G. Walsh OP

Liam G Walsh studied theology in Dominican Studia at Tallaght (Ireland), at *Le Saulchoir* (France), and at the *Angelicum* (Rome). He had Wilfrid Harrington as a valued colleague when he began his theological teaching in Ireland. He subsequently taught in Rome, and at the University of Fribourg in Switzerland. His writing has been mostly in the area of sacramental theology, and also on various aspects of the thought of Thomas Aquinas. He continues to teach at the *studium* of the Irish Dominicans in St Saviour's, Dublin.

Icons; iconographers

The four icons that feature in our pages were commissioned as part of the celebration of the 2012 International Eucharistic Congress, hosted in Dublin. One of these is featured at the beginning of each section of the book. The names of the writers are given here together with the title of each icon:

Our Lady of Refuge and St John (Philip Brennan), p 14;

Christ, Pantocrator (Richard Sinclair), p 30;

Elijah and the Raven (Colette Clarke), p 112 (and cover);

Pentecost (Colette Clarke), p 176.

Permission to reproduce these icons is gratefully acknowledged.